T0339948

The Lean Enterprise

The Lean Enterprise
Tools for Developing Leadership
in a Lean Culture

A. Heri Iswanto

Routledge
Taylor & Francis Group

A PRODUCTIVITY PRESS BOOK

First published 2021
by Routledge
600 Broken Sound Parkway #300, Boca Raton FL, 33487

and by Routledge
2 Park Square, Milton Park, Abingdon, Oxon, OX14 4RN

Routledge is an imprint of the Taylor & Francis Group, an informa business

© 2021 Taylor & Francis

The right of A. Heri Iswanto be identified as author of this work has been asserted by him in accordance with sections 77 and 78 of the Copyright, Designs and Patents Act 1988.

ISBN: 9780367488802 (hbk)
ISBN: 9780367488772 (pbk)
ISBN: 9781003043317 (ebk)

Typeset in Garamond
by codeMantra

To my loving wife, Shika,
and our children, Kannaya and Alfarrel

Contents

Acknowledgments

I want to praise the Almighty, Allah SWT, for the mercy and blessings I've been given so I could complete this book, *The Lean Enterprise: Tools for Developing Leadership in a Lean Culture.*

I extend special thanks to the colleagues who always give me motivation; my beloved wife, Shika Iswanto, who always supports me; and my dears, Kannaya and Alfarrel, who have been waiting patiently and gave their time until the completion of this book.

I realize that this book is still far from being perfect. However, I have performed my best in presenting it. Therefore, suggestions and criticism are always welcome for betterment. Finally, I hope that the book can be useful for professionals, practitioners, academics in general, and especially those who want to conduct and perfect similar research about Lean.

Author

A. Heri Iswanto completed his Doctorate of Economic Science majoring in Sustainable Development Management at Trisakti International Business School in the University of Trisakti, affiliated with Colorado State University (USA). He completed his Master's and Bachelor's degrees in Hospital Management in the Faculty of Public Health, University of Indonesia.

He works as an associate professor at Public Health in the Faculty of Health Science, University of Pembangunan National Veteran Jakarta, and as a lecturer at other universities in Jakarta. He has been the Senator Secretary of University, Vice Dean, and Dean of Faculty of Health Science.

He has also been director at various hospitals including Prikasih, Lestari, Kemang Medical Care, Budhi Jaya, and Ali Sibroh Malisi. He was an active speaker in many national and international conferences and has conducted trainings in the United States, Taiwan (Republic of China), IR Iran, Pakistan, Thailand, Malaysia, Singapore, Japan, Tiongkok/China, the Philippines, and Vietnam.

ESTABLISHING
CURRENT POSITION

I

Chapter 1

PDCA and A3

The starting point for implementing lean is to understand the current condition to be improved. Therefore, there are a number of ways that can be performed. First, we should understand the broad framework. This broad framework is called as PDCA (Plan, Do, Check, and Act/Adjust). PDCA provides the steps to be implemented as a whole in lean, but we put it in this section because understanding the current condition is the initial part of PDCA. Result of PDCA is manifested into A3 files. This file includes PDCA outlines. In identifying current condition, A3 contains identification of waste which consists of eight types. Identification of waste is performed by referring to the process map. Process map is at the bottom of organizational level. Second, we need to examine it to obtain a general description as well as a real illustration. Process map at the field level is referred to as value stream map. We have also learned an alternative format from the value stream map, namely the Swimlane map. Value stream map provides more complete information on time and process performance, but it cannot overcome the complexity of projects containing many decisions. Swimlane map describes the decision process that occurs among functions in the organization, so it can be a complement to the value stream map. There is also a spaghetti chart that illustrates the top view of a space layout.

How to make these maps? These maps are made by an initial observation called *Gemba* (process walk). Customer value is a guide to the activities of *Gemba* and maps preparation. *Gemba* is conducted through field observation while collecting the data of metric values considered as the customer value. The results of *Gemba* are included into process map, value stream map, Swimlane map, and spaghetti chart. Furthermore, more

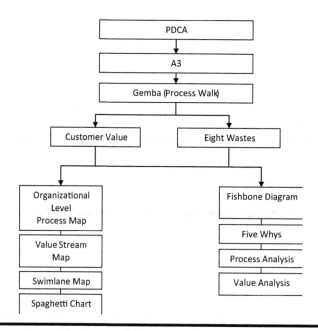

Figure 1.1   Framework of establishing current condition.

quantitative process analysis and value analysis of the map preparation are also performed. In addition, 5Ws (Five Whys) analysis is conducted, and fishbone diagram is prepared to find out the root cause of the problems found in *Gemba* and process analysis, value analysis, and mapping. The results of these processes will complete the steps in understanding the current condition. The chart in Figure 1.1 illustrates the correlation of these results.

We can consider this section as a part to understand the starting point of lean implementation comprehensively. This understanding is important because changing something without understanding the problem is just a waste of time. After all, this process of understanding is actually fun. The process of understanding the current condition includes understanding of the visual tool that allows us to see the functions of process that occurs, how to measure the effectiveness and efficiency of the process, determining tools to uncover root causes of the waste, understanding methods to determine the process value, and tools to understand as well as track the lean journey.

PDCA

PDCA stands for Plan, Do, Check, and Act/Adjust. *Plan* means determining goals, questions and predictions, and design to perform the address regarding who, what, when, and where. *Do* means organizing plans, recording unexpected problems and observations, and starting data analysis. *Check* means completing data analysis, comparing data with predictions, and summarizing what has been learned. *Act* means determining what changes must be made and the next cycle to perform (Moen & Norman, 2009).

As we know from the section on lean history, PDCA comes from the Shewhart cycle, which was later modified by Deming according to his observation on the implementation of the Shewhart cycle conducted in Japan (Moen, 2009). Therefore, PDCA is also referred to as the Shewhart cycle, Deming cycle, and PDSA (Plan, Do, Study, and Act).

PDCA needs to be run quickly, and therefore, it takes small steps. Planning does not need to be perfect because the point is learning from each cycle. This stage is conducted to prevent cessation of the cycle due to paralysis of analysis. Paralysis of analysis is a condition in which we expect that the results are perfect from the start, causing the cycle to remain at the planning point and stop progressing (Barandika, Beitia, Ruiz-de-Larramendi, & Fidalgo, 2013).

In the Check process, it is also necessary to examine parties that are affected, while supports are needed from various stakeholders by involving many parties. Managers must be present and involved in each cycle. Their presence is necessary to be maintained if unexpected consequences occur. Besides, it is necessary to plan tests on various process situations, so that natural process variations can be obtained.

The following details need to be considered at each stage of PDCA:

1. Plan

   At this stage, determine the issue to be raised and the current condition at hand. Involve other people in the health service team to determine problems and acquire background information as a support (Jagim, 2013). Agree on the objectives of the cycle and the expected outcomes of the testing cycle. Also, determine who will be involved and its term. Perform analysis to determine the root cause of the problem.

2. Do

   At this stage, develop steps to overcome the root cause that has been found. Coordinate and implement solution testing. Check if there are unexpected events during the testing. Record the deviations that have occurred since the initial plan.

3. Check

   At this stage, decide what works and what does not work. Compare the results with the expected results. Collect feedback from the participants of the process. Record everything that has been learned from the cycle.

4. Adjust/act

At this stage, if the results come out as expected, then plan to maintain sustainability. If the results are not as expected, use what has been learned to start a new PDCA cycle. Record the revised test plan. Plan the next cycle as an improvement step.

A3

A3 is a report format that was first developed by Toyota in the early 1960s to solve problems and provide continuous improvement. A3 report is structured into seven basic elements of (1) background, (2) current condition, (3) future goal, (4) root cause analysis, (5) countermeasures, (6) implementation plan, and (7) follow-up action. These elements are guided by PDCA (Saad et al., 2013). It can be seen that elements (1) to (5) are Plan, element (6) is Do, and element (6) is Check because it belongs to the implementation plan and the results of the implementation are written directly. Furthermore, element (7) is Act.

This report is called as A3 report because it is written on A3 (297 mm × 420 mm) paper. A piece of paper limits the amount of information, so that we can choose what is truly essential in this matter (Frøvold, Muller, & Pennotti, 2017).

The key to produce a good A3 report is *nemawashi* or a process to gain consensus (Bassuk & Washington, 2013). For this reason, it is important that all the relevant parties work together in compiling the A3 report, understanding it, and implementing it as a whole. A3 format is presented in Figure 1.2.

The following is an example of a more complex A3 format. In this example, A3 paper is divided into two columns. Plan is on the left side, consisting of problem statement, background/measurement, goal, current condition, and root cause analysis. Note that the goal is referred to as SMART. SMART stands for Specific, Measurable, Actionable (or Agreed upon), Realistic, and Time Bound. The bottom left side is a warning to stop. Before moving to the right side, the executor is required to meet with the stakeholders and those who perform this process to validate the left side and solicit ideas for countermeasures that later on will be listed on the right column (Figure 1.3).

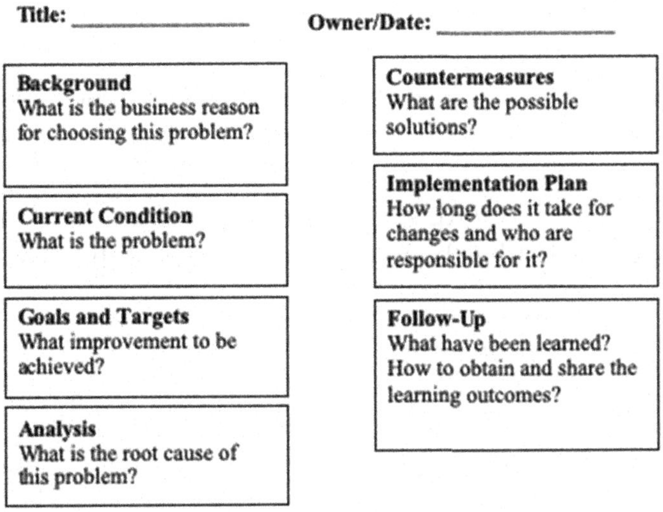

Title: _____   Owner/Date: _____

Background	Countermeasures
What is the business reason for choosing this problem?	What are the possible solutions?

Current Condition	Implementation Plan
What is the problem?	How long does it take for changes and who are responsible for it?

Goals and Targets	Follow-Up
What improvement to be achieved?	What have been learned? How to obtain and share the learning outcomes?

Analysis	
What is the root cause of this problem?	

Figure 1.2   A3 format.

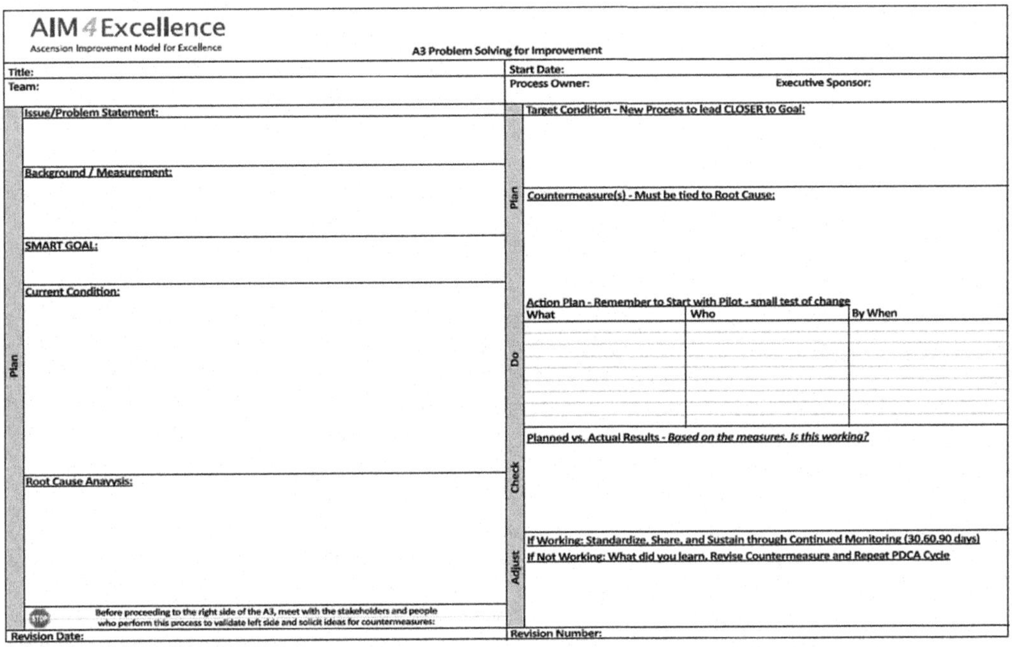

Figure 1.3   A more complex A3 example (Spivey, 2018).

On the right side of the paper, the Plan continues by listing the target condition in the form of new processes that will bring us closer to the goal, as well as a list of solutions that must be bound to the root cause. Next, the Do stage is in the form of action plan preparation consisting of what actions to take, who implements them, and when they will be performed. At this stage, keep in mind that the first action must be a pilot action which is a small test. The Check stage comes after the Do, in which the planned and actual results are presented. From this point, it can be concluded whether the plan works or not. Finally, moving to the Act stage, a decision is made. If it works, perform standardize, share, and sustain steps through continuous monitoring on 30, 60, and 90 days. If it does not work, revise the counter-measures based on what has been learned and repeat the PDCA cycle.

Chapter 2

Eight Wastes

The concept of waste is a broad concept and tends to be subjective. Therefore, it is important to define this concept. Realizing this, Hiroyuki Hirano defined waste from value aspect. According to Hiroyuki Hirano of Toyota, waste is "everything in the organization that does not process the product nor adds value" (Moreno-Sanchez, Tijerina-Aguilera, Aguilar-Villarreal, & Pilar-Tress, 2014).

At first, there were only seven wastes identified, namely overproduction, waiting time, unnecessary transportation, excessive or incorrect processing, excessive inventory, unnecessary movement, and defects. The experts then put forward the eighth waste. Many types of waste are proposed such as non-utilized skills and capabilities of human resources; non-utilized HR talent; goods design that does not meet user needs; unused potential human resources; lack of employees; unused creativity of employees; failure to use talents, skills, and HR capabilities; incomplete upstream operations; and resource polarization (Moreno-Sanchez et al, 2014). The eighth type of waste above is basically related to HR issues except for incomplete upstream operations. HR issues can be called as non-utilized talent. In line with this matter, the eight wastes were formulated into DOWNTIME, which means Defects, Overproduction, Waiting, Non-utilized talent, Transportation, Inventory, Motion, and Extra-processing.

Table 2.1 shows examples of eight wastes identified in outpatient pharmacy installation in PKU Muhammadiyah Hospital in Pekajangan (Putri & Susanto, 2017). This table also shows the correlation between waste and environmental impact (environmental waste), which also decreases the environmental performance of the outpatient unit.

Table 2.1 Waste at the Outpatient Clinic Pharmacy

Waste	Practice
Defects	Mislabeling, incorrect dosage written on prescription for patient because of similar packaging.
Overproduction	Pharmacy staff prepares medicine according to doctor's usual prescription prior to doctor's request.
Waiting	Pharmacy staff has spare time, especially morning shift staff, because doctors rarely have morning schedules or due to the delayed arrival of doctors. Patients have to wait for the pharmacy staff to perform administration process, drug check, and drug preparation.
Non-utilized talent	Pharmacy staff passively provides advice and comments to improve the service since management and other health workers such as doctors and nurses of the polyclinic do not provide an adequate response.
Transportation	Patient must travel to various places to get information about the next stage because there are no instructions or prior notifications.
Inventory	Supply of drugs is excessive; therefore, some of them expire, damage, or broken.
Motion	Pharmacy staff cannot move freely during work because of poor workspace management.
Extra-processing	Pharmacy staff must notify patients, especially Badan Penyelenggara Jaminan Sosial (BPJS) (Social Insurance Administration Organization) patients, because doctors give prescriptions which are not included in the national formulary, or prescriptions must be purchased at other pharmacies.

Source: Putri and Susanto (2017).

Another opinion states that DOWNTIME can still be used without the N, which stands for non-utilized talent. Rather than bringing HR issue into the form of waste, N is interpreted as Not Clear. It means that the eighth waste is unclear or confusing, so that it is harmful. Table 2.2 shows the application of DOWNTIME with the Not Clear component in medical context.

In the context of green manufacture, the eighth waste is the environmental waste such as air pollution, water pollution, soil pollution, and unnecessary use of resources. This waste is used to replace the HR waste. The relationship between the seven wastes and the environmental waste as well as their correlation to various elements is presented in Figure 2.1.

Table 2.2 Forms of Waste in Hospitals

Waste	Practice
Defects	Wrong drugs, rework, wrong billing, surgical errors
Overproduction	Multiple graphs, many forms with the same information, copies of forms sent automatically
Waiting	Waiting for employees at meetings, surgeries, medical procedures, reporting; patients waiting for meetings, doctor visits, medical procedures
Not clear	Similar activities performed differently by different people, unclear doctor orders, unclear drug administration routes, unclear system to indicate billing
Transportation	Drugs/supply delivery
Inventory	Excessive drugs, excessive supply in the unit or warehouse
Motion	Looking for information, looking for items, looking for people; items and tools are stored away from where they are used
Extra-processing	Clarifying orders, excessive information gathering, excessive document printing, missing drugs, tidying up paper

Source: Giacchetta and Marchetti (2013).

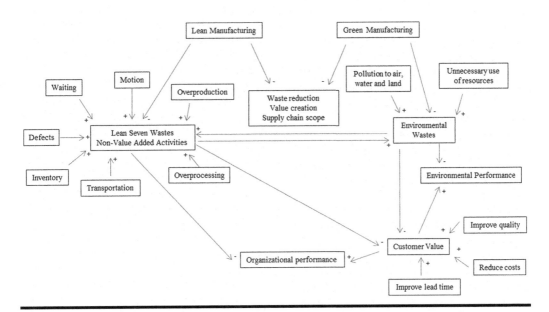

Figure 2.1 Dynamic model of lean green system (Hallam & Contreras, 2016).

Figure 2.1 shows seven wastes (overproduction, motion, waiting time, defects, inventory, transportation, and over processing) have negative effects on the organizational performance and customer value and cause an increase in environmental waste. Environmental waste also has interactive impacts on the seven wastes as well as causes decrease in environmental performance and customer value. Efforts to address these eight wastes will simultaneously increase the customer value as well as organizational performance and environmental performance.

Chapter 3

Organizational-Level Process Map

Organizational-level process map is the process map in an organization at the highest level. This map aims to explain the work of an organization. Map making is required to create a better alignment between various priorities, since in general, organizations are more focused on responsibility than process. They have organizational structures consisting of humans with different duties and responsibilities, but they do not have an organizational structure consisting of running processes in it. This kind of map will greatly depend on the type of organization and the product sold. However, the point is that this map must describe steps or processes that occur in an organization as a whole.

Value Stream Map Basics

Value stream map is created to make the work visible and graphically show all of individual steps needed to complete a process from the beginning to the end (C. S. Kim, Spahlinger, Kin, & Billi, 2006). This map is a visual presentation of the activities of service or product delivery from the customer's order to customer's hand (Fine, Golden, Hannam, & Morra, 2009).

The following is an example of value stream map from a study of Kim et al. (2006) in a hospital, related to the implementation of PICC (Peripherally Inserted Central Catheter) procedures.

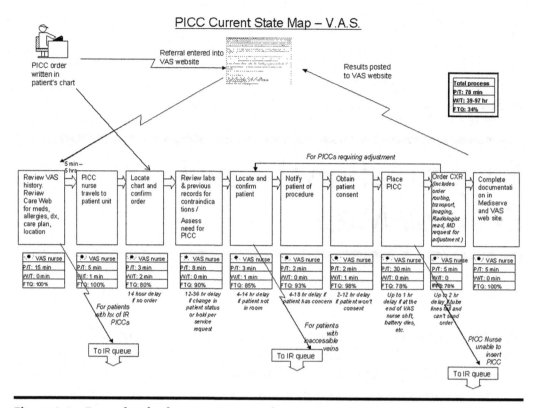

Figure 3.1 Example of value stream map of current condition (Kim et al., 2006).

Figure 3.1 shows how the process starts from the left corner. On the top left corner, PICC order is written on a patient's chart. This order is input on the VAS website (Vascular Access Services). In addition, orders also encourage staff to look for charts and confirm orders. From the VAS website, a review of VAS history is performed within 6 minutes to 5 hours. The review is performed to look for drug history, allergies, diagnosis (dx), treatment plan, and location. This process takes a process time (P/T) of 15 minutes. FTQ (First Time Quality) for this process is 100%. FTQ is the percentage of time in which the step is completed with no defect. 100% FTQ means there is no defect in this process.

After the review, the patient with hx PICC IR (Interventional Radiology) is admitted to queue at the IR. The nurse moves to the patient unit for 5 minutes with 1 minute waiting time (W/T) and 100% FTQ. The nurse then looks for the chart and confirms the order within 3 minutes, with 2 minutes waiting time and 80% FTQ. The FTQ is less than 100% because there will be a 14-hour delay if there is no order.

After the order is confirmed, the nurse reviews the laboratory and records of previous contraindications and assesses PICC needs. The processing time is 8 minutes with 90% FTQ. There will be a 12–36 hours delay if there is a change in patient status or the patient must wait per service request. After that, the nurse looks for and confirms the patient. The process time is 3 minutes, with 1 minute waiting time and 85% FTQ due to a 4–14 hours delay if the patient is not in his/her room. The patient, then, is directed to IR if the patient has an inaccessible vein.

Afterward, the nurse notifies the patient about the PICC procedure. This process takes 2 minutes, no waiting time, and 93% FTQ due to a 4–18 hours delay if the patient has problems. Subsequently, the patient gives the approval. This process takes 2 minutes, with 1 minute waiting time and 98% FTQ. There will be a 2–12 hours delay if the patient does not agree. Next, the PICC is placed. The PICC placement time is 30 minutes, with no waiting time, but the FTQ is 78% because there will be a delay of up to 1 hour if the procedure is performed at the end of the nurse shift, the battery dies, or for any other reasons. If the PICC nurse cannot input the PIC, the patient is queued at the IR.

After the PICC placement process, the nurse orders CXR (Chest X-Ray) that includes routing order, transport, imaging, radiological reading, and request for adjustment by the doctor. This process lasts 5 minutes with 0 minute waiting time and 78% FTQ due to the potential delay up to 2 hours if the line is full and the nurse cannot send the orders. If the PICC requires adjustment, the process returns to the step in which the nurse looks for and confirms the patient, explains the PICC procedure, asks for patient approval, and adjusts the PICC. If there is no more adjustment, the record is completed in the Mediserve and the VAS websites. This process takes 5 minutes, and the FTQ is 100% with no waiting time. The results then are posted on the VAS website.

In total, the process takes 78 minutes with waiting time up to 39–97 hours and FTQ only at 34%. The researchers perform corrective steps, and it is expected that this process can be slightly higher at 81–86 minutes, but it has only 7–10 hours waiting time and 88% FTQ. This is achieved through a process that will produce a future value stream map as shown in Figure 3.2.

In the new process as shown above, PICC needs are made by a doctor with 1 minute processing time and 30 minutes waiting time. The FTQ of this process is 100%. The doctor then orders PICC for 5 minutes, with 10 minutes waiting time and 100% FTQ. These results are posted on the VAS website. Needs are identified within 60 minute waiting time by the assistant.

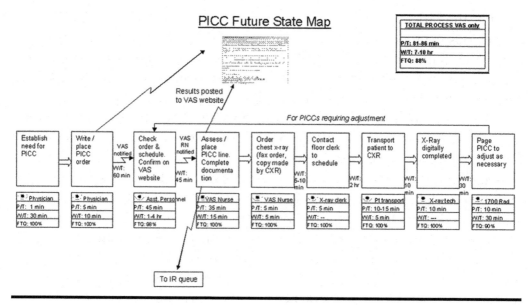

Figure 3.2 Examples of future value stream maps (Kim et al., 2006).

Assistant checks the order and schedule and confirms them on the VAS website. This process lasts 45 minutes with 1–4 hours waiting time and 98% FTQ. The nurse is notified within 45 minutes waiting time.

The nurse then assesses and places the PICC line as well as completes the record for 35 minutes, with 15 minutes waiting time and 100% FTQ. If the nurse cannot install the PICC, the patient is queued at the IR. Afterward, the nurse types the results on the VAS website. In addition, the nurse orders a CXR via fax machine. This process lasts 5 minutes, with 5 minutes waiting time and 100% FTQ. After 5–10 minutes waiting time to contact the X-ray officer, the X-ray officer then makes a schedule within 5 minutes and 100% FTQ. The transport officer sends the patient to CXR after 2 hours. This process takes 10–15 minutes with 5 minutes waiting time and 100% FTQ. The patient waits for 10 minutes, and the digital X-ray procedure is performed by an expert. The X-ray procedure takes 10 minutes with 100% FTQ. After 30 minutes waiting time, the results are obtained. The results are read by radiologists for 10 minutes with 30 minutes waiting time and 90% FTQ. If the PICC needs to be adjusted, the return process is repeated, starting from the assistant who checks the order and schedule for PICC adjustments. Note that FTQ in almost all steps reaches 100%.

The example of PICC procedure above shows how the value stream map can be used to monitor the overall process, various indicators that can be improved due to waste, and how the expected future state can be achieved.

Here is another example of labor case in a hospital. The first value stream map shows the patient's arrival, the patient enters triage, and the information is sent to the admin. This process takes 5 minutes. After that, the patient waits for 1–2 minutes and then registers. Registration takes 2–5 minutes. Here, the patient waits again for 15 minutes to 2 hours for assessment and treatment. Assessment and treatment of the patient are carried out in the delivery room. This process takes 1–13 hours. Furthermore, the patient will wait for one to two days before finally following the discharge process for 2–3 hours and finally goes home.

In Figure 3.3, the information flow at hand is poor because of unknown availability of delivery room and equipment. As a result, the waiting time is long, and the patient must go to another room, which is at a long distance.

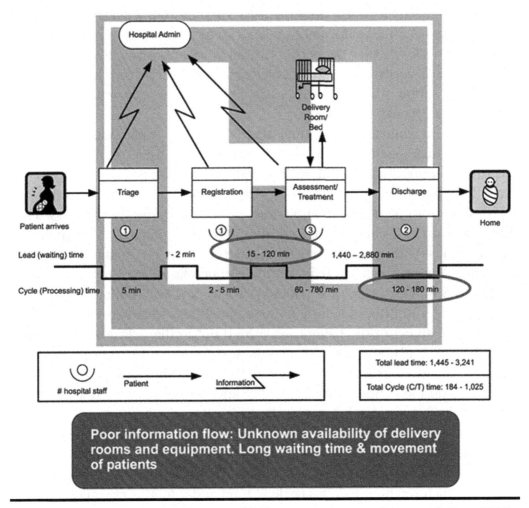

Figure 3.3   Current value stream map of labor process (Kumar, Swanson, & Tran, 2009).

The total lead time is 1,445–3,241 minutes (1–2.25 days). The total cycle time is 184–1,025 minutes (3–17 hours).

To overcome this problem, the research team installed RFID (Radio Frequency Identification Device). RFID is an electronic chip that is embedded in or very close to a product. RFID tracks the supply, equipment, people, or anything where it is embedded, so that it can find out the location of goods or people. Active RFID will continue to radiate signals in real time. Passive RFID is read only when a nearby scanner is placed. A special software manages data from the presence or absence of goods or people, so that decisions can be made immediately. For instance, RFID can be put on to patient's body, so that the capacity of the delivery room can be determined from the number of patients that is equal to the number of beds in the delivery room. Likewise, the presence of tools or equipment condition (good or damaged) to assist labor can be monitored immediately. In this way, the patient or nurse does not need to go in and out from one room to another to check whether the delivery room is vacant or not. RFID can also contain medical record data, so that electronic medical record data can be obtained by simply scanning or even just monitoring it. Consequently, the discharge process can be faster.

After the implementation of RFID, the future value stream map basically does not change much. No step is removed. Even so, there is an automatic and large amount of additional information flow between patients and hospital admin from the procedure room, delivery room, to ward. This information flow from RFID results in large time reductions during the process. The triage process takes only 2 minutes from the initial 5 minutes. After that, the patient just waits for at least 1 minute, rather than 1–2 minutes without RFID. Registration takes less than 1 minute, much faster than before which reached 2–5 minutes. Here, the patient just waits for 5–10 minutes, which was 15 minutes to 2 hours before, for assessment and treatment. Next, assessment and treatment of the patient are carried out in the delivery room. This process takes 1–13 hours. There is no change of time in this process because this is the standard process for dealing with labor and it varies greatly depending on the condition of the patient and her baby. Furthermore, the patient waits for one day before the discharge. The discharge process no longer takes 2–3 hours; it only takes half an hour to a maximum of 1 hour. The total lead time is 1,445–2,891 minutes (one to two days), and the total cycle time is 124–998 minutes (2–16 hours). It is lower than the previous process, which requires 1–2.25 days lead time and a total cycle time of 3–17 hours (Figure 3.4).

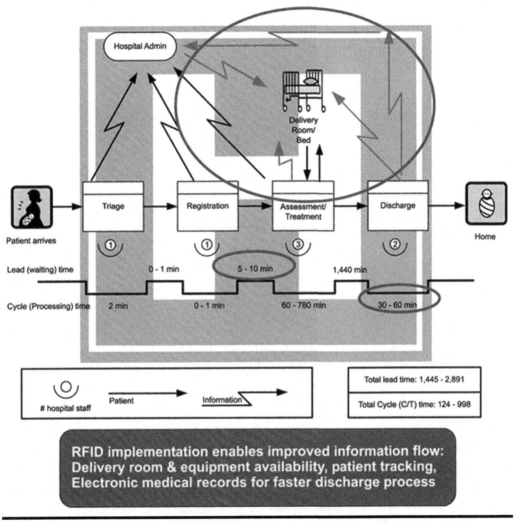

Figure 3.4   Future value map of labor (Kumar et al., 2009).

Swimlane Map

Swimlane map (including control chart, control plan, run chart, cross-functional process map) is a map that shows what steps need to be taken in a process and who is responsible for the process (Ojutkangas, 2016). Similar to the value stream map, Swimlane map can also describe the current condition as well as the future condition. Compared to value stream map, Swimlane map provides a more detailed description of the process; it can be used to find function transfer points, cycle time, and queues. It can be used for non-added-value activities within the process, and it contains decision points.

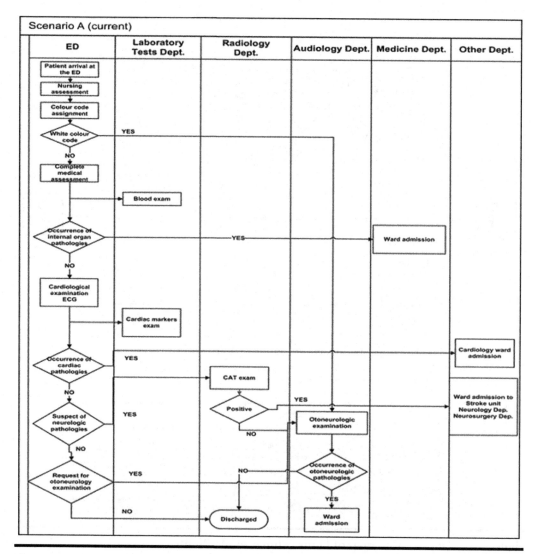

Figure 3.5   Example of Swimlane map (Celano et al., 2012).

Figure 3.5 is an example from Celano, Costa, Fichera, & Tringali (2012) who illustrate how Swimlane map is used.

In Figure 3.5, there are six departments responsible for the emergency of VSI (Vertigo Symptoms Illness) process. ED (Emergency Department) accepts patients; then a nurse conducts assessments and gives color codes. Patients with white code are referred to the audiology department for otoneurological examination, checked for the condition of otoneurological pathology, and submitted to hospitalization, if any. The patient may be discharged if nothing is found.

Patients who do not get white codes must complete a medical assessment in the ED. The department of laboratory test checks the patient's blood. The results of blood tests and other data are used to determine whether there is a pathology of internal organs. If the pathology is found, the patient is admitted to hospitalization and is under the responsibility of pharmacy department. If nothing is found, a cardiology examination with an ECG is performed. The Department of Laboratory Test examines cardiac markers. If there is a cardiac pathology, the patient is hospitalized for the treatment of a heart disease. If nothing is found, a neurological examination is performed. If there is a neurological pathology, a cardiac catheterization (CAT) examination is performed by the radiology department. If it is positive, then the patient is hospitalized in the stroke unit, nerve department, and neurosurgery department. If it is negative, the audiology department conducts an otoneurological examination. If there is an otoneurological pathology, the patient is hospitalized. If nothing is found, the patient is allowed to go home. A patient who is suspected of having neurological pathology is immediately examined for otoneurological pathology in the audiology department. If pathology exists, the patient is hospitalized. If not, the patient may be discharged.

The researchers then designed a Swimlane map that reduces the number of examinations for patient diagnosis and hence reduces time and costs. This Swimlane map is presented in Figure 3.6. In this map, patients with white code go through the same path as the previous. However, patients with other colors can immediately go through clinical assessment and brain abnormal diffuse perfusion examination.

If a patient does not have an abnormal brain diffuse perfusion, the patient is immediately referred to the audiology department for otoneurological examination. If there is a pathology, the patient is hospitalized. If a pathology is not found, the patient is examined for neurological pathology. If a pathology is not found, the patient may go home, but if there is a pathology, the patient should undergo a CAT examination. If the CAT is positive, the patient is admitted to the stroke unit. If it is not, the patient may complete a medical examination, including blood tests in the laboratory. If there is an internal organ pathology, the patient is hospitalized. If there is no pathology, the patient may be discharged. A patient with abnormal brain diffuse perfusion is then examined for ECG with cardiac markers. If there is a cardiac pathology, the patient is hospitalized for the treatment of a heart disease. If there is no pathology, the patient is treated as usual.

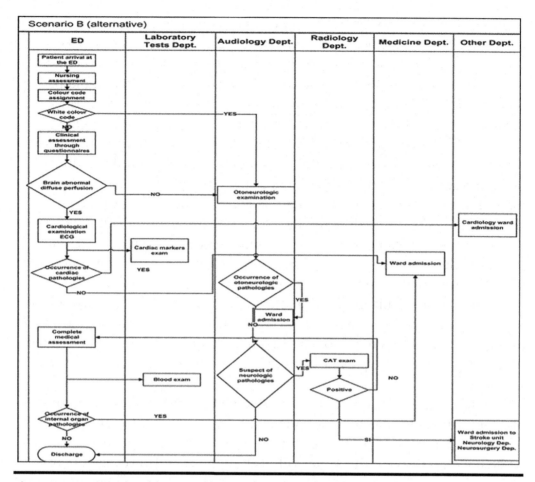

Figure 3.6 Example of future Swimlane map (Celano et al, 2012).

Process Walk

Process walk or *Gemba* is an activity to observe the actual process in the organization, step by step. Three things done during *Gemba* are as follows: making observations and discoveries, looking for potential opportunities, and looking for potential solutions.

This activity is important to make a value stream map. If it only relies on the testimony of others, the process that occurs can be biased or can come only from a limited perspective. The process is considered to take place in one version or one point of view. In the field, it turns out to be more complex. This is very likely because everyone is focused on one area (silo) in a larger process. The existence of function-based management through functional/departmental management in the organization creates these silos.

In some aspects, function-based management is good. However, there are fundamental differences between a process and a function. A process shows the sequence of activities performed for a particular purpose, while a function is the management of activities in certain fields of knowledge or expertise. Most processes involve activities with various functions. A number of weaknesses caused by function-based management include the following (Cox, 2002):

1. No one feels that they have or need to optimize the process to see the critical relationship among them because roles and responsibilities are determined in relation to functional requirements. This means the strategic focus of the process is hindered. The scope and schedule of certain activities can also be problematic with the overall needs of the process.

2. The process is managed and developed incrementally, based on the needs and interests of individuals who have certain functions, rather than based on the needs of customers who are at the end of the process. It happens because no one has a sense of ownership to the process. Each department tries to optimize its own performance which can sacrifice the performance of the whole process. Competition between departments will emerge instead of cooperation and knowledge sharing to optimize the process.

3. There are only a few people who understand the whole process where they work. Few people understand how their actions in their department affect the whole process. This can only be seen clearly if there is a cross-functional team which serves to analyze and improve the existing process.

4. Performance measurement in an organization is directed at functional performance measurement rather than process performance. There is only a few metrics that really measure the effectiveness and efficiency of the process the customers went through because the focus is on the efficiency of the department.

5. Many problems arise at the point of interdepartmental encounter. When it happens, departments blame each other. Such problems include inconsistent practices and duplication of activities.

6. *Gemba* makes the perspective of management shift to a product- or process-based management rather than a function-based management. It removes departmental egos that frequently occur both in public service institutions and private organizations. With *Gemba*, people get

an idea of who the customer is and get a perspective from the whole chain of actions and the point of entry, so that the product or service is obtained by customers and they understand how they must act to meet the needs of these customers.

In Japanese, *Gemba* means "the actual place". This place in the context of lean-based health services can be in the form of an ED, outpatient dialysis unit, or surgery room. Before making a value stream map, the participants performed *Gemba* to see the value and process that made it. This matter departs from the view that values that patients want are created at the frontline, not in the boardroom (Fine et al., 2009).

Gemba provides many benefits in improving quality. First, *Gemba* provides a lot of knowledge about the current condition of the process. The current condition can be mapped. In fact, even small, simple tasks can be performed, such as mapping tools which are not available on the table or determining machines with a long processing time.

Second, *Gemba* confirms or destroys the assumption about how the process is happening. Third, with *Gemba*, we can gain an understanding of the whole process, rather than just understanding each part of the process. An employee in one department might wonder what happens in another department of the process. With *Gemba*, they get a direct view of what he/she assumes, and his/her suspicions can be answered.

There are also broader benefits than just the immediate benefits above. *Gemba* is able to increase knowledge transfer in an organization because the team as a whole collaborates. They communicate with each other, and their abilities to solve problems are increasingly visible. As a result, mutual trust begins to grow among *Gemba* team members and between *Gemba* team and process actors. The team will also increasingly understand the process as a whole and learn the importance of data and quality. This reflects an increase in the organization's capacity to absorb knowledge and internalization of knowledge. Organizational ties grow, and the familiarity between teams and process actors gets better (Siren, 2008).

Sunder (2016) stated the benefits of *Gemba* as follows:

1. It provides first-hand direct information about problems in the process to the project manager.
2. It provides co-workers with psychological benefits because with *Gemba*, managers show the colleagues that they are important in the progress of the organization and they play critical roles in the process.

3. It saves time to learn new processes.
4. Reveals hidden wastes in processes which are not generally identified through advice or data analysis.
5. It understands the root cause of the problem if the process actors are asked the right questions and there is a learning process from observation. This is because process actors are the ones who work on the process every day, so they really understand what is in and out of the process.

Imai outlined ten benefits from the Gemba-based problem-solving activities for an organization. These benefits include the following (Sung, 2018):

1. The needs of *Gemba* can be easily identified by people who work in their position.
2. People who are in the process always think of all kinds of problems and solutions.
3. Barriers to change are minimal.
4. Continuous adjustment is possible.
5. Solutions based on reality can be obtained.
6. Solutions raised emphasis on reasonable matters and low cost, rather than expensive and method-oriented approaches.
7. People can enjoy it and be inspired by it.
8. Awareness of solutions and work efficiency can be increased simultaneously.
9. Workers can think about solutions at work.
10. It is not always necessary to require approval from top management to make changes.

Spaghetti Diagram

Spaghetti diagram is a visual illustration that shows a process. It aims to understand the layout and its effect on the process, so that steps to change the layout to reduce wastes can be performed. Figure 3.7 is a spaghetti diagram from Bahensky et al. (2005).

The diagram on the left illustrates the current condition of the process a radiology technician went through. Here, the technician moves from the door to get the patient ready and then takes the patient to the scan room. The technician then goes back to the control room and finally takes the

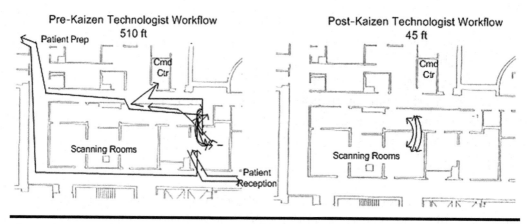

Figure 3.7 Example of spaghetti diagram (Bahensky, Roe, & Bolton, 2005).

patient out. The total distance traveled is 510 ft. After repairing, the technician goes back and forth from the scan room to the waiting room without dropping or taking the patient and coming back to the control room. The reduction achieved is 91%, in which the distance traveled is only 45 ft per patient.

Customer Value

A customer is a person or an organization who gets a product or service (output) from work (process) performed by a product/service provider. A customer can be within the organization or an external customer. An internal customer is a recipient of work completed by upstream specialists (previous process), while an external customer, also called end customer, is a customer who gets the entire product or service produced from the entire team of specialists in the process (Y. Kim & Ballard, 2002).

Patients are examples of external customers. Nurses or physicians who are involved in a process are customers of the previous process. In general, especially clinical staff (health worker), customers are only seen to include patients because they are the parties who receive treatments. Even so, the clinical doctors who provide referrals to the hospital are also customers, so are the regulators and the internal departments of the hospital.

Customer value is what customers want. The concept of customer value is defined as "the overall assessment of the customer toward the utility of a product based on perceptions of what he/she deserves and what he/she gets" (Oh, 1999). Customers have requirements for the products and services provided, so these requirements need to be known in order to meet and provide the desired customer value. Therefore, before running lean, it must be confirmed what value is needed, expected, or desired by customers. Hospitals need to understand or determine this value from patients and other customers. This must be seen from the perspective of the patient's path from their entry to the hospital until their discharge. Failure occurs if the understanding of customers and customer values varies between departments or stages of value stream (Radnor, Holweg, & Waring, 2012).

Examples of values that may arise from patients are access, quality, affordability, responsiveness, flexibility, hospitality, speed, comfort, convenience, and accuracy. The research by Aghlmand, Lameei, & Small (2010) carried out at a maternal and children hospital reveals customer value through interviews as well as based on degrees ranging from the most important to the least important including the following (Aghlmand et al., 2010):

1. Baby's welfare.
2. Mother's welfare.
3. Labor with mild pain.
4. Careful and responsive staff.
5. Frequent monitoring.
6. Privacy during labor and vaginal examination.
7. Quick response on request.
8. Labor and childbirth education.
9. Provision of comfort.
10. Listening to the baby's heartbeat.
11. Normal labor.
12. Accompanying during delivery.
13. Opportunity to see the newborn baby.
14. Replacing bed linen frequently.
15. Good hospital facilities.
16. Painless vaginal examination.
17. Short labor.
18. Assisting mother in breast-feeding.
19. Clean delivery room.
20. Discharge from the hospital as soon as possible.

For this reason, organizations need to listen to the VOC (Voice of the Customer). In addition, voices from their business, process, department and stakeholder also need to be considered. This can be obtained directly (interview, discussion, or survey) or indirectly (complaint, behavior, market analysis, or observation). These voices are then translated into measurable indicators to be achieved by a lean process.

To ensure that the lean process has taken into account customer value, a customer value checklist can be used. Table 3.1 shows a customer value checklist.

Table 3.1   Customer Value Checklist

Customer Value Checklist		
Field of Work: _____		
#	Question	Action
1	What is our core process?	
2	What is the main thing we give to customers?	
3	What are our key sub-processes?	
4	Who are the key customers of these processes?	
5	What is important to customers in this process?	
6	How do we measure what is important to our customers?	
7	Do we track what is important to our customers?	
8	If yes, how well do our core processes work on customers' requirements?	
9	Are our assumptions about what customers want true?	
10	What are the specific requirements about what customers want?	
11	How do we continue to be in harmony with our customers and the requirements of these customers?	
12	What are processes and indicators that have strategic meaning?	
13	Which process is the most painful for customers?	
14	Which process has the most expensive rework?	

Chapter 4

Lean Metrics

There are many lean metrics that can be used to understand a process. Commonly used metrics include the following:

1. Process Time (P/T) is the time used to run a process.
2. Waiting Time (W/T) is the time used to wait before the process starts.
3. Lead Time (L/T) is the total process and consists of process time and waiting time.
4. Work in Progress (WIP) is the number of items on the work waiting list.
5. Percent Complete and Accurate (% C/A) is the time percentage of an input received with complete and accurate information.
6. Changeover Time (C/O) is the time needed to shift from one activity to another and is also called as setup time.
7. Takt time is the ratio between the net of working time available to customer demand. Takt comes from German which means rhythm. Takt describes the required production steps to meet customer demands. This metric is important to understand how quickly the process must run in order to be able to meet customer demands.
8. Lean metrics collection is performed by involving voluntary health workers at the hospital. It is performed by using an interview form that is collected through the process walk (*Gemba*). Actually, the interview is just a simple data collection form designed for ordinary transactional/office processes. Even so, the form facilitates to remind what questions need to be asked when conducting a process walk or *Gemba*. *Gemba* is a journey performed by the lean team to the process floor from one point to another to observe the process in real time. One form must be

completed for each step of the process. Create a time path on the value stream map with cycle time data on this form for each step of the process. The process interview form is presented in Table 4.1.

Process Analysis

Process analysis is the analytical step needed after the process map is determined. The analysis examines opportunities that might exist in a process. In addition, process analysis examines the possibility of repetition, waste, and bottlenecks. Process analysis is also able to understand how inspections can produce rework.

Process analysis may include the following steps (Nnamdi, 2015):

1. Evaluate the significance of a particular step. This evaluation, for example, whether there is any repetitive step which is unnecessary, there is any value added in the process, and so on, is used to remove the redundant steps, improve quality, and reduce cost.

Table 4.1   Process Walk Interview

Process Walk Interview		
Interviewer: _____ Interviewee: _____ date:		
Step #:	Process Step Name:	
# staff:	# shared resources:	% time available:
Lead time:	Work time:	% complete and accurate:
# unit in a box (WIP):	Setup time (if applicable):	Information flow:
Batching:		
Flow constraints or wastes in this process step:		

2. Investigate delay or symbol of delay or time lag in the step.
3. Focus on too many areas of specialization and handoff. Excessive exchanges increase the potential for mistakes.
4. Investigate the decision points, namely key inputs and outputs.
5. Observe the quality control points and rework loops.
6. Investigate the overall process or comprehensiveness of the existing map, such as logical flow, process sequences, repetitions, bottlenecks, and disconnections.
7. Check the costs to run the process.

In addition, it is also necessary to measure rework. Measurement of rework needs to be performed to estimate the amount of costs incurred for rework. This knowledge allows efforts to remove or eliminate the costs of rework and therefore improve cost performance in the process (Simpeh, 2012).

Rework is different from the design iteration because rework is unwanted. Rework may occur due to changes in criteria, data errors, data loss, analysis errors, and discrepancies among production intentions (Tribelsky & Sacks, 2010). Rework index is measured as the proportion of information that changes in the developed total information (added or changed) between the two steps of the process. Mathematically, the rework index (RWI) is formulated as follows:

$$RWI = \sum_{i=1}^{nIO} \left[\frac{nIA_T^r}{PS_T - PS_{T-1} + nIA_T^r} \right]$$

PS is the package size, and nIA_T^r is the number of information attributes whose values have changed in the period between T and $T-1$ (Tribelsky & Sacks, 2010). Another way to measure rework is by using the floor size where the rework was performed (Holweg, 2007).

Value Analysis

There are several methods to optimize value stream in order to reduce waste, namely value engineering (VE), value analysis (VA), design structure matrix, and so on (Mujtba, Feldt, Petersen, Mujtaba, & Ab, 2010). Value analysis is a common step taken to optimize the value stream after mapping the initial condition and measuring the process steps (Dickson, Singh, Cheung,

Wyatt, & Nugent, 2009). The value of customer's perspective is determined in value analysis. There are three types of value-based activity:

1. Value-added activities are activities or process steps that are considered valuable by customers. The main characteristics of the activities or process steps that add value are as follows:
   a. The customer is willing to pay for it or at least paying attention if he/she has to.
   b. Changing items toward the final product or service.
   c. Must be performed correctly since the first time.
2. Non-value-added activities are activities or process steps that do not add value from the customer's point of view.
3. Value enabling, or activities that are necessary but do not add value are activities or process steps that are still seen as non-value-added activities, yet they are considered necessary to run a business, for example, activities to ensure compliance with laws and regulations.

The step taken for value analysis is finding waste by identifying which steps add value and which ones do not. After waste is found, waste ranking is performed based on the experience of frontline employees. The output of value analysis is a redesign process in which the focus is directed at how to get a future condition or ideal condition (Dickson, Anguelov, Vetterick, Eller, & Singh, 2009).

Five Whys and Fishbone Diagram

Five Whys (5Whys) is a root cause analysis method by questioning "why" to a problem up to five levels. This method is adopted from Toyota and continues to be an important part of lean.

5Whys are important because they can reveal hidden effects from a distant cause. Taiichi Ohno compares 5Whys with 1 H (how) since a solution can be obtained (how to) after knowing the root cause of the 5Whys process (Card, 2017). An example of 5Whys is as follows (Arnheiter & Maleyeff, 2005):

1. The problem is passed the deadline. Why?
2. Long lead time. Why?
3. Not enough capacity. Why?
4. Long setup time. Why?
5. Adjustments are very time consuming. Why?

5Whys is recommended in health service sector by WHO and many other national and global health institutions. However, Card (2016) observed that a problem in the health sector can have many root causes, and hence, 5Whys must not be seen as an absolute solution to solve a problem. For example, take a look at the three following 5Whys examples. These three examples look for the root of the same cause but produce two different root causes.

A. Problem: wrong medication for patients
   1. Why? Wristband is not checked.
   2. Why? Wristband is missing.
   3. Why? Wristband printer in the unit is broken.
   4. Why? Label is stuck.
   5. Why? Poor product design.
B. Problem: wrong medication for patients
   1. Why? Wristband is missing.
   2. Why? Wristband printer in the unit is broken.
   3. Why? Health-care system purchased unreliable printer.
   4. Why? Process of evaluating and purchasing non-clinical equipment is bad.
   5. Why? Equipment that is deemed as non-clinical is not considered critical for patient safety.
C. Problem: wrong medication for patients
   1. Why? Patient with the same name in the same room.
   2. Why? Do not have time to arrange patient's bed.
   3. Why? Lack of nurses in dealing with too many patients.
   4. Why? Nurses are affected by nanovirus outbreaks.
   5. Why? Poor compliance to infection control intervention that takes a lot of time.

Because of this weakness, 5Whys is not recommended for issues related to patient safety. 5Whys can only be used for matters involving factors or human interaction and daily business activities. In other words, 5Whys is only effective on simple problems, and hence, for complex problems, 5Whys needs to be combined with other techniques because complex problems often have several interdependent root causes (Jones, Medlen, Merlo, Robertson, & Shepherdson, 2000).

For more complex problems with many root causes, fishbone diagram can be used. Fishbone diagram is a diagram in the form of fish bone, in which the head illustrates the problem, while each bone segment is the

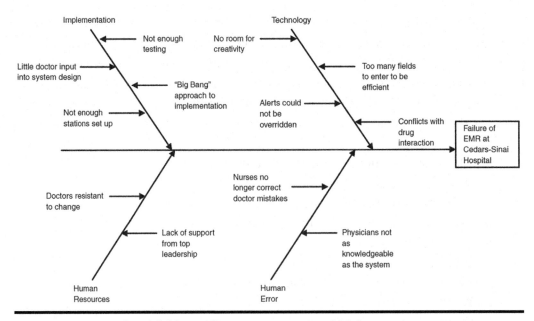

Figure 4.1   Example of fishbone diagram (Kumar & Aldrich, 2010).

factor causing problems. For more details, Figure 4.1 is an example of a fishbone diagram by Kumar & Aldrich (2010) in the case of electronic medical record failure in hospital.

In Figure 4.1, there are four groups of factors that cause failure of electronic medical records at Cedars-Sinai Hospital, namely technology, human error, implementation, and HR. Technological factors are as follows: no room for creativity, too many fields to fill to be efficient, alerts cannot not be overridden, and conflicts with drug interaction. Human error factor includes nurses who are no longer correct, the doctor's mistakes, and doctors who are not as knowledgeable as the system. Implementation factor includes insufficient testing; there is a little input from the doctor to the system design, sudden approach to implementation, and insufficient station setup. HR factor includes doctors who resist changes and lack support from the leaders.

Another example of fishbone diagram usage can be seen in Figure 4.2. In this figure, the root cause of rework on hospital design is presented. It is pointed out that rework has five root cause groups, namely HR capabilities, leadership and communication, engineering and review, construction planning and scheduling, and supply of materials. HR problems include contracts, overtime, unclear instructions to workers, inadequate skill levels, insufficient supervision, insufficient work planning, and accidents and emergencies (A&E). Leadership and communication problems include unclear

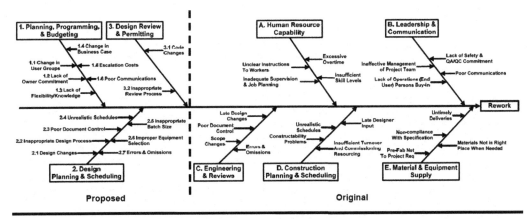

Figure 4.2 Example of fishbone diagram in accidents and emergencies department (A&E) (Feng & Tommelein, 2009).

master facilities plan, absence of target costs, lack of safety and quality assurance/quality control commitments, ineffective management of project team, poor communication, lack of operations support from end users, different interpretations of regulations, and unauthorized construction. Engineering and review issues include late design changes, scope changes, fire problems, lifesaving, safety, poor file control, errors and omissions, changes of ownership, and seismic requirements. Root causes of construction are planning and scheduling including unrealistic schedules, late designer input, constructability issues, insufficient turnover, insufficient commissioning resources, space constraints, safety, lifesaving, and fire problems. Root causes of material and equipment include untimely deliveries, medical equipment changes, non-compliance with specification, materials not in the right place when needed, and pre-fabricated materials not being according to project requirements. Some of these types of problems may not appear in one case and may appear in other cases. Therefore, it is necessary to examine which root causes actually arise in a problem of hospital redesigning.

Figure 4.3 is a sample of a fishbone diagram for the case of the telemedicine challenge. Within this framework, outcomes from the implementation of telemedicine in the form of cost effectiveness, service quality, and patient satisfaction are determined by six groups of factors, namely service provider, organization, society, patient, technology, and rules. Problems from service provider are solved by workflow and expertise on ICT; by patient communication, education, and training; and by provider interaction and resistance to change. Organization problems include leadership, organizational

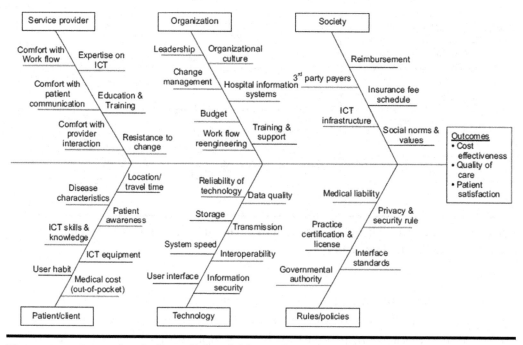

Figure 4.3 Example of telemedicine fishbone diagram (Chang, 2015).

culture, change management, hospital information systems, budget, training and support, and workflow reengineering. Challenges from the society include reimbursement, payments from third parties, insurance fee schedules, Information and Communications Technology (ICT) infrastructure, and social norms and values. Challenges of rules/policies include medical liabilities, privacy and security rules, practice certification and license, interface standards, and government authority. Technology challenges include reliability of technology, data quality, storage, transmission, system speed, interoperability, user interfaces, and information security. Challenges from patient or client include location/travel time, disease characteristics, patient awareness, ICT skills and knowledge, ICT equipment, user habits, and medical (personal) costs.

DEVELOPING
FUTURE POSITION

Chapter 5

Developing Future Position

In this chapter, we will discuss about the solution to improve the current situation, so that we can achieve the expected results. It is the step after the root cause is identified in PDCA (Plan, Do, Check, and Act/Adjust) process. Various techniques discussed in this chapter are strategic since they can be chosen according to the type of problem.

In general, this chapter consists of three parts. The first part discusses how implementation is performed. There are number of ways to manage implementation: quick win, quick fix event, pilot, and multi-phase implementation. Multi-phase implementation consists of quick win, quick fix, and pilot. Multi-phase implementation can be called as a common implementation management method, while quick win, quick fix, and pilot are specific types of implementation. The starting point for all these activities is a future state map.

This chapter also discusses a number of quality improvement techniques that can be performed in quick win, quick fix, and pilot activities as well as multi-phase implementation. These techniques include one-piece flow and batch reduction, changeover reduction, work cell design, workload balancing and demand lifting, cross training, *Kanban* and supermarket, standard work, visual management, foolproof, and 5S. Finally, after each goal has been achieved, we arrive at the last part, the pursuit of perfection. Correlation of these concepts is shown in Figure 5.1.

One-piece flow is the movement of material or information through a step-by-step process without WIP (Work in Progress) within the existing steps. This indicates that there is a small batch at all times. One-piece flow

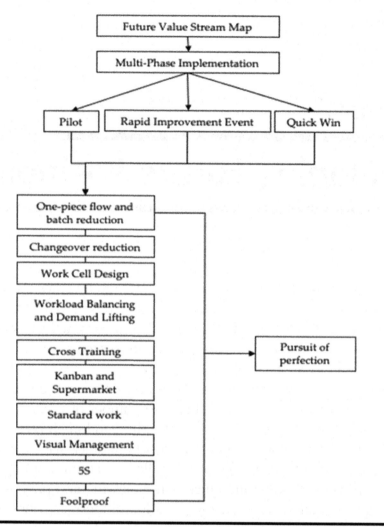

Figure 5.1 Framework of developing future state one-piece flow and batch reduction.

is opposed to large batch processing at a time, or also called batch-and-queue method (Arnheiter & Maleyeff, 2005), which also means there is an accumulation of request or order in one box.

At first, it seems that the use of many batches at the same time is efficient. However in reality, handling multiple batches at the same time actually slows down the process, and consequently, it increases cycle time. This is because each step will take a long time to run, and when the entire process has been completed, there are many products available which may exceed the demand, resulting in buildup. On the other hand, the next process cannot run and must wait until the first process is completed in a long time (Ward & McElwee, 2007).

Batch size reduction can be achieved by arranging process steps in a natural sequence. Batch reduction will in turn minimize cycle time and travel distance. In addition, handoff becomes minimum, and internal consumers have a closer relationship with the suppliers.

Changeover Reduction

Changeover is the period between the last good product from the previous production sequence that leaves the machine and the first good product out of the next production sequence. Working in small batches results in frequent changeover. In fact, changeover is not desirable because this process is time consuming and increases the time wasted in searching, walking, waiting, missing tools, non-standard work, poor schedule information, and no calibration. Therefore, changeover reduction will increase flexibility and maximize bottleneck capacity, so it maximizes the availability of production lines and maximizes equipment effectiveness, leading to production cost reduction (Ferradás & Salonitis, 2013).

The common method for changeover reduction is SMED (Single Minute Exchange of Die) (Bevilacqua, Ciarapica, De Sanctis, Mazzuto, & Paciarotti, 2015). SMED divides setup operation activities into two categories: (1) internal activities performed when the machine is offline and must be minimized because it slows down production, and (2) external activities performed when the machine is running. SMED works by reducing the time spent on many changeover steps by performing as many activities as possible when the equipment is running and simplifying as well as streamlining the remaining steps. It allows a smoother production flow. Improvement is carried out by separating external and internal changeover steps, changing the internal to external if possible, simplifying internal steps, reducing or removing adjustment requirements, and streamlining external steps.

Work Cell Design

Cell design is a method of managing physical operations in the most efficient combination to maximize steps that add value and minimize waste. In this case, the waste targeted is the waste of motion, transportation, and waiting time. The result of cell design is a small cycle time and simpler process. Cell design in a manufacturing system, such as drug manufacture, often becomes the first step to achieve lean production (Tohidi & Liraviasl, 2012).

Cell design arises because the work often takes place in isolated islands in a standard department layout. Processing with these isolated islands creates queues and hence results in increased cycle time. Increased cycle time is due to the excessive movement of materials, parts, and products inside and among the islands (Gunasekaran, Mcneil, McGaughey, & Ajasa, 2001). A good work cell produces a sustainable flow which minimizes queue and increases cycle time.

The benefits of good cell design include (1) simpler prioritization and communication, (2) fewer resources used among steps, (3) provision of feedback and resolution of problems quickly due to increased visibility, (4) employee understanding toward the process so as to improve process knowledge, (5) shorter cycle time, and (6) demand adjustment leading to small batches.

Workload Balancing and Demand Lifting

Workload balancing is to maintain a fixed direct load for each machine or capacity group (Fernandes & Carmo-Silva, 2009). Workload balancing is important because imbalanced workload will cause some machines or groups of capacity to remain inactive during the process which in turn will slow down the process. If the machine or group capacity remains active, the process will be more efficient. If the process is more efficient, the process speed will be faster. Mathematically, workload balancing is a case where the level of operator utilization, which is the ratio between the operator's actual workload and its capacity, is balanced (Yalcindag, 2014). It is a balanced workload distribution for all input reflected by the alignment of input waiting time (Haneyah, Hurink, Schutten, Zijm, & Schuur, 2011).

The indicator of workload balance is time in system. Time in system is the time a job spends waiting in the pre-shop pool plus the shop flow time. Shop flow time is the time that elapses between job release and job completion.

Workload balancing has several benefits, including the following (Fernandes & Carmo-Silva, 2009):

1. It reduces overall response time for consumers.
2. It reduces capital needed to produce products or services.

Workload balancing is needed in sub-processes to adjust to the demand efficiently, so that every process is always on time and keeps running.

The process must be kept in line with the takt time (consumer demand). This is achieved by redistributing resources and jobs. It not only adapts to time but also helps in keeping the inventory in check. Workload planning is an important element in the standard operating procedure (SOP) of an organization (Sobanski, 2009).

If the process has a wide variety in the volume of demand, workload balancing cannot solve the problem. The step that can be taken is by lifting the demand at the low demand volume. Demand lifting is an attempt to increase demand through modification to certain processes that can affect how demand comes from customers.

Demand lifting causes the demand to be uniform and unvarying. This facilitates the work management. An example of demand lifting is giving discounts on small volume days and avoiding demand when the volume is high. Demand lifting is also a part of workload planning (Maarleveld, 2015).

Cross Training

Cross training is conducted to train the employees to perform other work within the organization's work. According to Hopp & Van Oyen (2003), cross training provides benefits including the following:

1. It reduces worker cost by increasing workers' productivities. This happens in three ways:
   a. Cross-trained workers can perform more work during scheduled business hours. In other words, the use of human resources increases due to the greater flexibility.
   b. Cross-trained workers can work faster, for example, through the establishment of cross-trained working teams who are able to exploit the synergy among them, so that work can be completed more quickly.
   c. Increased flexibility allows the system to reduce investment in WIP and/or inventory.
2. Cross training allows shorter lead time and more reliable delivery by reducing average cycle time and its variation in manufacturing a product or service. This is achieved by reducing congestion, so that the average cycle time is shorter. Congestion reduction is achieved from increased worker flexibility, combined with the increased task speed, reduction in setup and handoff times, or minimization of variations in task completion time.

3. Cross training supports better internal quality that improves external quality and reduces the frequency of entity exchanges by allowing the system to develop greater capabilities so as to provide better ways to meet the customer needs. Examples of internal quality improvement are reduction in losses and reduction in rework. An example of an increase in external quality is compliance with consumer-oriented product specifications.
4. Cross training can increase organizational flexibility and therefore help in providing a more effective range of products and/or services. This is achieved by equipping workers with a large number of skills, so that they can do more, and providing job redundancy, so that the system can provide diversity more reliably. For instance, if a worker is absent or taking a break, another worker can do their work to produce the desired product or service for a consumer.

In addition, cross training indirectly does the following (Hopp & Van Oyen, 2003):

1. It supports learning by enabling workers to be faster, more organized, or more reliable over a long period of time.
2. It enables communication which helps workers coordinate their tasks better. For example, cross training of upstream workers to do downstream job can improve their ability to communicate the information to downstream workers who facilitate the work of the upstream workers.
3. It facilitates problem solving by making worker more responsible to each type of work. For example, finding better work methods, diagnosing the causes of quality problems, and improving team-based *Kaizen* initiatives.
4. It provides motivation to increase the level of effort and cooperation by giving workers a broader organizational perspective.
5. It increases worker retention through job satisfaction, compensation, and/or the development of career path.
6. It improves performance because the ergonomic effects of jobs' variety are greater. One of the examples of ergonomic effects is eliminating fatigue, boredom, or stress due to working on the same thing over and over again.

The various benefits of this cross training are illustrated in Table 5.1.

Table 5.1   Benefits of Cross Training

Purpose	*Direct Mechanisms*	*Indirect Mechanisms*
Cost	Higher labor productivity: Increasing the use of labor Increasing the use of resources Increasing work speed Reducing WIP and inventory	Learning Communication Problem Solving Motivation Retention Ergonomics
Time	Increasing responsiveness: Increase in work speed Increase in capacity flexibility Reduction in working time variation Reduction in setup and handoff times	
Quality	Improving internal/external quality: Increase in suitability of labor/work Customer service improvement Fewer handoff entities	
Diversity	Broader product/service offer: Greater scope of work Increase in production flexibility	

Source: Hopp & Van Oyen (2003).

Cross training provides a clearer understanding and shared representation (shared mental mode) related to how the organization functions and how the duties and responsibilities of each employee are interconnected (Wilson, Burke, Priest, & Salas, 2005). According to Wilson et al. (2005), there are three types of cross training:

1. Positional clarification is general knowledge of related positions and responsibilities.
2. Positional modeling is knowledge and training related to general dynamics of the process, tasks of other employees, and how the assignments relate to and affect the duties of others.
3. Positional rotation is work knowledge about others' specific work activities and how the task interacts with and affects others.

In the health sector, cross training is important. For example, nurses who have joined cross training can substitute other nurses who are absent because of illness or help them if they need help (Wilson et al., 2005). In addition, health workers who get cross training will become more valuable and feel less boredom.

Chapter 6

Kanban and Supermarket

Kanban is a mechanism for controlling the flow of material that controls the quantity and appropriate time for the production of goods (Phumchusri & Panyavai, 2014). Kanban is a system using a card or other visual instructions to give a sign of a need to produce or deliver a container of raw materials or semi-finished materials to the next stage in the manufacturing process (Worley, 2004). Kanban is used to improve efficiency, effectiveness, and flexibility of manufacturing in accordance with the consumer needs. It guarantees the right product at the right time and the right amount at the right place. This is better than the push system which tends to have higher operational costs than the Kanban system (pull system) (Adnan, Jaffar, Yusoff, & Halim, 2013). Kanban-based scheduling also reduces inventory, smooths flow, prevents overproduction, and controls operational levels; procurement schedule and management processes can be easily seen visually, and they have responsiveness to demand changes, have less risk of inventory failure, and have better ability to manage supply changes (Ikonen, 2011). Other benefits mentioned in the literature include a better understanding of production process, improved product quality, increased compatibility between consumer needs and customer satisfaction, increased employee motivation, improved communication/coordination between stakeholders/work groups, quicker improvement of defects, increased productivity, problem solving (easier problem detection and solution), batch size reduction, reduced shipping time, increased frequency of release, more efficient and controlled projects, easy implementation of changes in specifications, quick feedback without delay, no need for documents in large number because it is limited to consumer demand, and no requirement for management approval since the approval is obtained from consumers (Ahmad, Markkula, & Oivo, 2013).

The concept of Kanban is often juxtaposed with the concept of supermarket. The supermarket discussed here is not a store we can find in everyday life, but it is a concept describing the placement of the final product from the Kanban process. Even so, both are related. In fact, the basic idea of Kanban is derived from the logic behind supermarket operation in America. Ohno observed that the shelves in supermarket were only refilled when consumers bought products. Ohno then made it the same as the previous and subsequent processes not only in the service industry but also in the manufacturing industry (Malavasi & Schenetti, 2017).

Kanban and supermarket are used to order internal supplies. Kanban and supermarket can be used if there is a reserve of work in the process among workstations (Bortolotti, 2010). In the Kanban system, each stage of the production line has a set of cards (Kanban). Certain cards are attached when one part arrives at one stage and are removed after the part has left the stage. If a card is still attached, no other part can enter the stage. When the part leaves, the card is taken and attached to the new part. This makes Kanban an internal inventory control system (Román, 2009).

Meanwhile, supermarket is a final product placement from a certain stage. Supermarket serves to find out how many items have been produced. If the product leaves the supermarket, this means that there will be more products to be made. The amount of Kanban sent to the provider of items and empty space in the supermarket have the same function, which determines the supply to be filled (Roman, 2009). The previous process should only be made if it has received Kanban from the previous process or if there are empty spaces in the supermarket (Waren, 2013).

In this way, supermarket acts as a buffer against variations in demand. If Kanban rigidly sends requests one by one and production items one by one, it could be that a queue will occur if there are many sudden requests. For this reason, it is necessary to provide several items at once on the shelf which is a supermarket model, so that variations can still be overcome. This amount should not be too much because it will lead to a similar situation to a push system which makes Kanban ineffective. Only if the shelf is empty, the Kanban is sent, and the production process starts again to fill the shelf completely. It means that Kanban without a supermarket produces only one product if there is a demand and Kanban combined with a supermarket produces several products at a time. As an illustration, Kanban and supermarket systems are discussed in the following example.

There is a shelf that can hold the same four drugs, let's say paracetamol. In the initial condition, this shelf is empty. The officer of the shelf sends the production Kanban to the warehouse. The warehouse sends four paracetamols to the shelf. One consumer comes and buys one paracetamol. Because of this purchase, the officer of the shelf sends a withdrawal Kanban to the warehouse, asking the warehouse to make one paracetamol. On the shelf, there are only three paracetamols. Then, the consumer comes to buy again, the withdrawal Kanban is sent again, one new paracetamol is made in the warehouse, and there are two paracetamols on the shelf. Next, the third consumer buys one paracetamol. The same process repeats. There is another fourth consumer who comes, and the shelf is finally empty. When the shelf is empty, the officer at the shelf sends not only a withdrawal Kanban but also a production Kanban to the warehouse. The warehouse makes one more paracetamol. The warehouse now has four paracetamols, and they are sent to the shelf. The shelf is full again.

In fact, the existing system is longer. Figure 6.1 provides an example of how Kanban works on goods that experience three processes: process A, process B, and process C. In each process, there is one supermarket. Goods coming from suppliers are then stored in supermarket as raw materials; then they are taken to process A, stored in WIP (Work in Progress) supermarkets, then taken to process B, stored in WIP supermarkets, then brought to process C, and finally stored as the final goods of the supermarket. Consumers come and take one product, Kanban is sent back to the supplier, the supplier sends one raw material to supermarket, and so on.

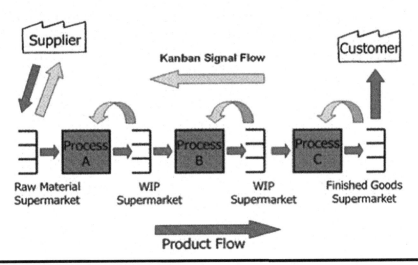

Figure 6.1 Flow of Kanban and supermarket processes (Bracket Smack Down, 2019).

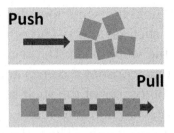

Figure 6.2 Difference in principles of push and pull systems (Kanban) (AllAboutLean, 2015).

In this process, the final product shelf is always full in which the principle of "first come first out" applies. This is actually not too different from filling the shelf when the shelf is empty. As far as there is WIP limitation, whether it is one or four or whatever according to shelf capacity, this system can be seen as a pull system. In push system, WIP is not limited, or in other words, WIP is infinite.

From the description above, determining the number of containers on the shelf is critical. Too many containers can result in many expired items if there are only a few buyers. Too few containers can cause queues because there are too many consumers and they have to wait. To determine this, an experiment needs to be conducted first to determine the right shelf size to serve consumer demand without causing waste of time or inventory. Note that the experiment is chosen here, not market forecasting as in the push system. Market forecasting focuses on logistics plans that estimate consumer needs rather than actual needs. Experiment, on the other hand, is based on real situations in the field. Machine production capacity may not be optimal if there is little demand, but this is better than maximized machine production capacity that results in too many items piling up without a buyer (Figure 6.2).

Chapter 7

Standard Work

After a new method that is able to increase value has been created, this change must be maintained. Maintaining it is a challenge. The solution to maintain this new way is to create standardized jobs. It means that when a most efficient and effective way is formed, it must be a standard work. In other words, the new process continues with the new standard operating procedures (Holden, 2011). This standard work is developed and then continuously improved by the employees who do the work (Ben-Tovim et al., 2008). Standard work applies not only to the employee level but also to the top level and leadership (Mann, 2009).

For this reason, it is important to perform standard work documentation. Standard work documentation allows employees to see the processes around them. It is manifested in work instructions. However, standard work in lean is different from standard work in the world of the Tayloris (non-lean) industry. Standard work in lean is written by employees who perform it, while Tayloris standard work is written by company staff to be performed by the employees. Ohno saw that if standard work is written by staff, they sometimes do not know why an action has to be taken. They do not have real experience with work and standard work; they wrote standardization is likely to be rarely followed by employees who know better reasons for one work order (Nakane & Hall, 2002). The standard compliance theory states that when standards made from the external are forced, it may lead to the hypocritical implementation, which in turn leads to cynical resistance, and finally the compliance is only demonstrated as a symbolic compliance (Sandholtz, 2012).

In a lean system, standard work is made by employees because they understand the steps to do the job (Nakane & Hall, 2002). Then, the manager serves to provide ongoing support for a sustainable standard work documentation activity (Yee, Zain, & Sin, 2017).

Standard work documentation is achieved by developing process documentation. Development of process documentation relies on the success of documentation as well as the effective use of resources. The forms of documentation can be either process flow chart or process map. The stages of process documentation are shown in Figure 7.1.

The steps above are explained as follows:

1. Select the process to be documented.
2. Determine the purpose why this process must be mapped, i.e., whether it is only to describe or to improve the process.
3. Determine the level of detail. The process documentation should not be too detailed. It must be easily understood, yet not too simple to allow improvement of process.

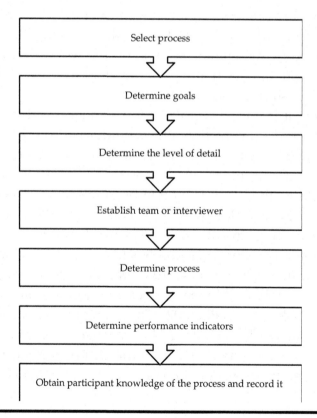

Figure 7.1 Stages of process documentation (Bengtsson & Sjoblom, 2006).

4. Establish a team or interviewer. This is in line with the methods used in collecting the process data. If the scope of the process is small, interviews can be selected, and therefore, data collection requires an interviewer. If the process is complex, extensive, and involves many components and workers, data collection is performed in teams in various ways whether it's simulation, observation, or other means. Both the team and interviewer must possess in-depth knowledge of the process.
5. Determine the process. After the team or interviewer is selected, then the process is defined. This definition is important to limit what is the scope of the process and what is not. Knowledge of this process will include inputs, outputs, participants, and so on.
6. Determine performance indicators. Performance indicators are used to determine whether the process under study has a good or bad performance.
7. Collect participant knowledge of the process and record it. This is the data collection stage. After the data is collected, re-examination is performed to identify whether the documented process is correct or there is still something missing or wrong. All parties then review and agree upon the final documentation.

The documentation of the above process then is reviewed and examined to find what can be corrected. After improvement ideas emerge and are implemented, there will be a better process. This improvement step is then recorded in the standard work instructions and operation sheets. The improvements will result in changes to standard operating procedures or create standards if indeed there is no standard operating procedure at first. This standard must be documented and tested. Employees need to be trained to carry out this new procedure. For this reason, a curriculum is needed to provide training both theoretically and practically. These three things – work instructions, standard operation sheet, and training – are the parts that support standard work (see Figure 7.2). After training, the implementation of standard work is performed. Even so, the implementation of standard work needs to be performed after the production process is stable and shows consistency.

This implementation in turn needs to be audited to ensure success. To ensure adaptation, it must be ensured that the employee is aware of the new procedure. If the employee understands that, check whether they use the new procedure. It also needs to be seen whether there are regulations imposed to make sure that the new procedure is obeyed. For this reason, a

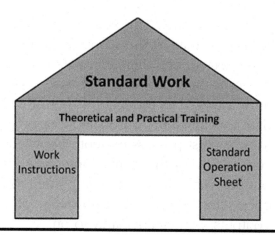

Figure 7.2   Standard work pillars (Ribeiro, Alves, Moreira, & Ferreira, 2009).

Table 7.1   The New Procedure Audit

Procedure Name	Observed Level								
	Awareness Level			Usage Level			Enforcement Level		
	Date	Date	Date	Date	Date	Date	Date	Date	Date

tool called The New Procedure Audit can be used to perform a new standard implementation audit. The New Procedure Audit can be seen in Table 7.1.

Each cell under the date in Table 7.1 can be filled with three possible values namely H (high), M (medium), and L (low). Of course, other metrics models can also be used, for example, 1, 2, and 3 or a range of scores from 1 to 10, depending on the agreement. In short, from Table 7.1, it can be seen that there is a change from time to time in awareness, usage, and enforcement of certain applied standard rules. For example, see Table 7.2 on the standard work of pediatric radiation therapy floor nurse by Austin (2015).

Table 7.2 shows the situation of audited work standards at three different times, which is on March 16, April 25, and June 5. There are many parties involved in pediatric radiation therapy. It includes anesthetists, anesthesia

Table 7.2 Example of Application of the New Procedure Audit

Procedure Name	Observed Level								
	Awareness Level			*Implementation Level*			*Enforcement Level*		
	16 Mar	25 Apr	5 Jun	16 Mar	25 Apr	5 Jun	16 Mar	25 Apr	5 Jun
Complete the preoperative checklist	M	M	H	L	M	M	M	M	H
Verify the time for patients to leave the unit and meet an ambulatory procedure technician or anesthesia/respiratory technician in radiation therapy	H	H	H	H	H	H	M	M	M
Report to the nurse an ambulatory procedure at least 20 minutes before the scheduled treatment	L	H	H	L	H	H	M	H	H
Report to the nurse an ambulatory/anesthesia staff procedure about fasting time, changes in status, level of pain, respiratory problems, and completion of the preoperative checklist	M	H	H	M	H	H	H	H	H
Take the patient to the cancer center for radiation therapy treatment (after the initial patient report to the preoperative provider for anesthetic consultation and parental consent)	L	M	H	L	L	H	H	H	H

technicians, ambulatory care nurses, child life specialists, floor nurses, interpretive officers, nurse coordinators, pediatric radiation oncologists, respiration care practitioners, radiation therapists, radiation therapy nurses, schedule organizers, and unit nurses. Each one has their own standard work that needs to be audited. In this case, the auditors are floor nurses. These nurses have five standard work tasks as registered in the procedure name.

On March 16, the audit found that the nurse had low awareness on two procedures, medium on two procedures, and high on one procedure. At that time, there were three procedures run with low, one with medium, and one with high awareness. The level of procedure enforcement at that time was classified as medium, and two were already high. In the audit on March 25, the nurses no longer had a low awareness of their standard work tasks. There were two points that were still classified as medium. Meanwhile, for the implementation, there was only one procedure that was run low. The procedure enforcement level was still the same as that of the previous audit. During the audit on June 5, awareness of all procedures was high. There was only one medium procedure implementation, while the others were already high. Enforcement also got better because there was only one that was classified as medium.

After the audit is completed, if indeed to be performed by a specially established team, then this team needs to be dissolved with proper recognition by a letter for legitimate (Chang, 2007). The results obtained by implementing standard work are analyzed and discussed by managers and all the elements involved in the project. From here, the main lessons are taken, and reflections are made about the results of the project (Braganca & Costa, 2015).

Chapter 8

Visual Management

Visual management is a step to find out errors in the system. Visual management, visual workplace, visual control, or visual tool is a management system that tries to improve organizational performance through the use of visual stimuli to highlight, clarify, report, and integrate vision, mission, value, and culture into operational systems and organization performance requirement (Bwemelo, 2016). Visual management builds communication with executors using one or more visual devices that can provide, signal, or limit information. This visual device includes, for example, visible objects, lists, and graphics. This allows a place or a particular tool or policy to be self-visualized, self-arranged, self-organized, and self-improved (Bwemelo, 2016).

Visual management is important to improve quality because it provides an opportunity to monitor instant improvement every day. Visual management allows tools, goods, and processes to be easily observed, so that everyone can find out whether there are normal or abnormal situations (Terfie, 2018). In other words, visual management makes the performance of each workplace and work team transparent. In addition, visual management visualizes standardized operations and processes (Pries, 2004). In relation to the improvements that have been made, the essential of visual management is to make all aspects of the process that will be and have been improved become apparent.

The principles of visual management are quite widely stated in the literature. These principles include affordable, mobile, easy to understand, updated information, flexible in relation to user needs, accurate, financially plausible, able to mitigate problems related to system complexity, contribute to cultural changes in organizations, designed to simplicity of function, adjust the mental model of the designer and user, and have a behavior-oriented approach to achieve the target (Valente, Pivatto, & Formoso, 2016). These principles can in turn be simplified into four principles as follows:

1. Simple. The visualization displayed is easy to understand. The use of words is efficient in every visual. Simple also means avoiding waste because it uses the least number of symbols to get the most effective message.
2. Large. The visualization is in large size so that it can be easily seen. Small writing is efficient in space but makes it difficult to read.
3. Visible. Visualization is made in a place where people can easily see it.
4. Changeable. Visualization allows the people who see it to make changes to it.

Take, for example, the use of a single standard worksheet for the head department. This worksheet is equipped with "Check invoice" feature to facilitate the comparison of invoices provided by employees with internal documents so that it is easier to see errors (de Koning, Verver, van den Heuvel, Bisgaard, & Does, 2005). Another example is a specially designed chart that is then reviewed at each weekly meeting. This graph shows the OT (operating theater) start time from the previous week. Feedback from this meeting is then used to monitor the OT start time continuously so as to provide valuable input in improving the existing process (de Koning et al., 2006).

In line with this, there are four steps to use visual tools which are given as follows:

1. Identify units and materials. Visual tools of this function are addressed to clarify the contents of a particular container or area, so that people no longer need to search for the items. They can find out where to look for something by just glancing it without having to open the lid from the container (Figure 8.1).
2. Inform people about the status of the process. In this case, a visual instrument takes the form of a large board in which there is space for regular discussion and shows critical information. There are pieces of stationery – markers and erasers – nearby to update the situation. Examples of this visual management are shown in Figures 8.2 and 8.3.

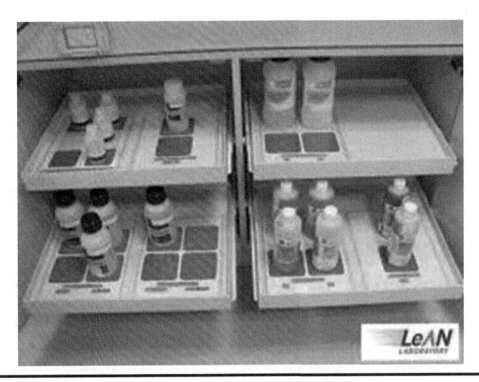

Figure 8.1   Placement of unit and material with markers (Novartis, 2019).

Figure 8.2   Example of wall with visual management (Lindsey, 2017).

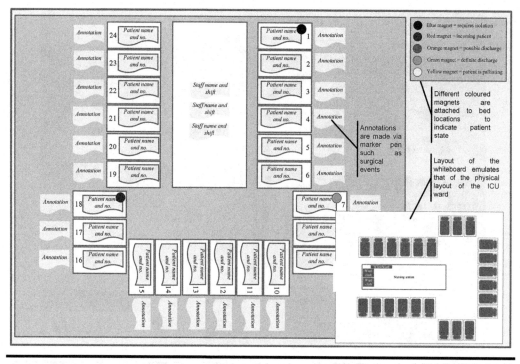

Figure 8.3 Example of visual management for ICU patient status (Beynon-davies & Lederman, 2017).

3. Instruct people on how a process works. In this case, visual management is performed by providing step-by-step instructions, placing arrows on the floor or wall to indicate the process flow, indicating on the floor where a device should be placed, and including pictures of part, material or equipment in it. Figure 8.4 shows the visual management function to instruct people about how to properly place medical devices by attaching the symbol of the device on the floor where the device should be stored.

4. Display the ongoing plans. In this case, visual management has a role to show how the process is going on, so that people know what their responsibilities are and provide the latest updates to the plan (Figure 8.5).

The effectiveness of visual management to improve quality is explained through affordance theory (Beynon-davies & Lederman, 2017). According to the theory, human physical environment is structured; i.e., the properties of the structure are not arbitrary. Human perceives these physical structures directly without conscious and cognitive intermediary processes.

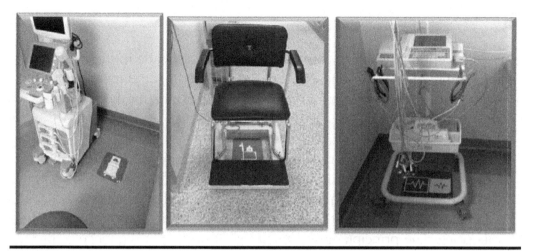

Figure 8.4   Visual position of storing medical devices (Miller, 2009).

Figure 8.5   Example visual progress of a plan (Regina Qu'Appelle Health Region, 2015).

This perception then provides a limit or convenience for humans to act. How easy or difficult humans' act is due to perceptions of this physical structure depends on the effectiveness of humans themselves, as seen from the sensors and effectors. Sensors are sensory organs such as eyes, ears, nose, tongue, and skin. Effectors are organs that allow humans to change the environment, such as hands and feet. Visual management is a structure in the environment which can then be seen by someone with his/her eyes even unconsciously without having to think. This vision then encourages a person to act with the effector.

5S

5S is a concept that was first formalized by Takashi Osada in the early 1980s (Young, 2014). 5S is a five-phase technique for building and maintaining a quality environment within an organization. 5S stands for the following (Young, 2014):

1. Sort. This means categorizing items in a work environment. Sorting can be carried out based on frequency of use or by product types, for example, intravenous equipment, respiration, and elimination.
2. Straighten/set in order. The aim of straightening is to put everything in its place. The principle is to arrange work items in a sequence of processes related to work and place the number of items in accordance with the requirements so that it will be easier and faster to take items such as intravenous devices.
3. Shine/scrub. Its purpose is to clean all areas. Frequently, the back area is the most rarely considered part of the hospital. Clean everything so that things that could potentially bring safety problems can be easily and quickly identified.
4. Standardize. Standardization aims to apply visual techniques to make work fields with the same function look the same. Coloring the boxes, for example, is a form of visual management that can establish standardization. Place the product family in different color boxes, such as yellow for intravenous, red for wound care, green for elimination, blue for respirator, orange for personal care, indigo for personal protective equipment, and purple for other items.
5. Sustain. It aims to create a well-maintained work environment in the long term. This involves documentation and usage of metrics. The work team must follow the standard work guidelines and manage standard information boards. Supervisors keep documents and measure metrics for conducting sustainability evaluations.

5S implementation in the context of health services provides a number of benefits to the work environment, staff attitude and behavior, patient attitude and behavior, as well as service quality. Tables 8.1 shows a number of benefits from 5S (Kanamori et al., 2015).

5S can be further developed by integrating inventory management techniques and process improvement tools, as long as they are relevant to the goals of 5S. The example in Tables 8.2 shows the differences between applying traditional 5S and hybrid 5S (Venkateswaran, 2011).

Table 8.1 5S Benefits in Health Service

Domain and Sub-Domain	Benefits
Work environment	Fewer unwanted items Hygiene and cleanliness improvement Increase in items' regularity Improvement of labeling and service unit direction indicators
Staff attitude and behavior	Increase in 5S awareness Increase in collaboration between staff members Increase in reuse of items Extension of 5S practice beyond work
Patient attitude and behavior	Voluntary participation in maintaining cleanliness of facilities
Service quality	
Efficiency	Reduction in time to search for items Increase in staff capacity to move in the office
Focus on patient	Reduction in patient waiting time Better direction for patients
Safety	Improvement in sterilization process

Source: Kanamori et al. (2015).

Table 8.2 Application of 5S and Hybrid 5S

Steps	Traditional 5S	Hybrid 5S
Pre-Work	Circles of work Experience-driven inventory management	Spaghetti map Circles of work Redesign strategy Historical usage-driven inventory model
Sort	Removing obsolete or rarely used supplies	Removing obsolete or rarely used supplies
Set-to-Order	Visual enhancement Ergonomics enhancement Grouping similar items Creating signage to clearly label items and aisles Creating new catalogue to improve ease of access for end users	Grouping of supplies based on ABC classification Analyzing space requirements for supplies. Placing the shelves in their designated places Labeling items in their new location Labeling "A" category items on each shelf

(Continued)

Table 8.2 (*Continued*) Application of 5S and Hybrid 5S

Steps	Traditional 5S	Hybrid 5S
	Consolidating locations to ensure each supply has only one storage space	Providing a clear representation for each shelf
Shine	Creating a cleaning mechanism	Floors and aisles free from oil or dust Cleaning the shelf Providing sufficient lighting
Standardize	Standard work document which states the problem, action taken, and its results	Report at the end of each day Reordering quantities based on inventory model Visual management of supplies exceeding the space allocated
Sustain	30-day action plan to maintain results	Periodic check on "A" category materials 30-day action plan to maintain results

Source: Venkateswaran (2011).

Future State Value Stream Map

Previously, it was explained that VSM (value stream map) could be made for current and future states. Future VSM is used to guide the achievement of improvement objectives. Measure of improvement can be assessed based on whether it has been achieved or not by looking at the future VSM and the results of assessment. Figure 8.5 shows how a complete improvement process must occur and be achieved by the executors of the lean program.

Chapter 9

Quick Wins

Quick Wins or Just-Do-It is a change solution which focuses on possible improvements with a little effort but great benefits (Redzic & Baik, 2006). Quick Wins involve one or two people for implementation, and it can be implemented in less than two weeks, does not involve many fields or departments, and has support from the leadership and participants of the process. Solutions that are classified as Quick Wins, however, might look simple but are actually more complicated. They could have unexpected impacts on other fields or functions, could be rejected unexpectedly, and could use resources and cause delays. Therefore, it should be ensured that the solution proposed is really Quick Wins.

However, the Quick Wins solution must be selected carefully. Overuse of Quick Wins will only lead to short-term improvement, and the situation in the near future will return to the comfort zone. To prevent this situation, a systematic lean approach to change the work culture is more likely to provide long-term results (Guimaraes & de Carvalho, 2013). Lean failure is often caused by the application of continuous Quick Wins without considering the long-term changes (Radnor, Holweg, & Waring, 2012).

Rapid Improvement Event

Rapid Improvement Event (RIE) is a quick improvement activity that occurs over a longer and more complex time than Quick Wins. RIE aims not only to achieve improvement, but also to instill changes in work culture and to achieve sustainable transformation. RIE solves problems faster when compared to the routine meetings.

RIE lasts for around one to five days to one week depending on the purpose. In certain cases, it can take up to several weeks. For example, RIE with the aim to improve patient travel can last one week. If the aim is to improve the working of radiology services, establish trauma stabilization units with significant input from doctors, manage the process in the operating room, discharge of patients, and cross-disciplinary group cooperation, it will last for six weeks (Fillingham, 2007). Individuals involved in RIE work sequentially at the design and/or implementation stages.

RIE consists of planning, execution, and follow-up activities. The work in each stage is as follows:

1. Planning: At this stage, the information and required data are collected. The team then determines the scope of activities. Furthermore, the team attracts support from the key stakeholders. After gaining support, the team prepares participants, logistics, and supplies for implementation.
2. Execution: The execution stage begins with the preparation of agenda and objective. After that, a schedule is arranged. Once it is ready, the implementation is executed. After the completion, the participants carry out the plan.
3. Follow-up: This stage is performed for 30, 60, and 90 days after execution. The purpose is to communicate and report to the interested parties.

As an illustration, the following is the case of holding RIE at Abernarle Home Care (AHC), North Carolina, United States. AHC faced a problem because it had to make a daily schedule to take care of patients in their homes after surgery or hospitalization. AHC decided to solve this problem with an RIE. A cross-functional team of nine people was formed. These nine people consisted of nurse staff, nurse team leaders, billing coordinators, patient admissions staff, and outside observers. An RIE was planned to last for four days. The stages carried out include the following (Smith, Poteat-godwin, Harrison, & Randolph, 2012):

1. Day 1
   a. Short lean training is carried out by two lean health specialists.
   b. The team conducts a process review through *Gemba* walk so that the team can see the actual process which eventually makes them understand how the process functions and identifies the waste activities.

    c. After *Gemba* finished, the team gathers and identifies 38 waste items.

    d. The team creates a value stream map of the scheduling process and lists waste items on the map.

    e. The team identifies three areas as the focus of improvement: first, the quality of information that comes to reception staff; second, the issues and delays faced by staff in the field serving patients; and third, reduction of the time needed to make daily assignments so that the staff nurses can immediately meet the patients.

    f. The team is divided into three sub-teams.

2. Day 2

    a. Each sub-team works independently to generate ideas, test changes, and validate those ideas, so that they know which ideas are successful and which are not. For example, there is a team member who carries a hanging shoe rack from home to be used as a container of completed work, so that the nurse staff can immediately work on the field and meet the patients quickly.

    b. The sub-teams meet to report on each other's results and findings and discuss new improvements and ideas.

    c. Directors and key staff members meet with the teams to discuss progress. This opens up the communication and prevents the team from misleading in working.

3. Day 3

    The processes on the third day are the same as those of the second day, which are as follows:

    a. Each sub-team works.

    b. The sub-teams gather and discuss the results.

    c. The team designs a new system. This system revises the placement data, sorts the information when the call comes, removes the need to sort and find information during the morning meeting, consolidates patient files used in the field by nurses, and modifies the filing process.

    d. The team discusses the results with the director and key staff members.

4. Day 4

    a. The team implements a new communication system.

    b. The team prepares the next RIE.

    c. The team applies 5S to improve the health supply space for home health and storage.

5. Follow-up: In the next 90 days, the team meets regularly to complete items that are still unresolved.

Based on the RIE above, the team observes that they have achieved progress in both the visible and invisible ones. This progress includes (Smith et al., 2012)

1. Invisible progress
   a. The three nurse leaders are free to conduct better supervision tasks.
   b. The nurses have more times to spend with their patients.
   c. Organizations are more profitable because they serve more patients with the same number of staffs.
   d. Paper costs, time, and fax costs are reduced.
   e. Nurse staff visiting patients early can complete daily targets on time, have computer time after less field work, and can start working directly from home without having to go to the hospital to take a schedule.
   g. Greater staff work spirit.
   h. The acceptance process is smoother with better resource allocation.
2. Visible progress
   a. Scheduling time decreases from 60 minutes to 20 minutes.
   b. Nurse expenses reduce by 20%.
   c. In the first year, there is an increase in the number of visits to patients treated at home by 4% with the same number of staff.
   d. The first semester of the second year shows an increase in patient visits by 8%.
   e. In certain regions, the number of visits even increases by 18% from the initial 3.79 visits per day to 4.49 visits per day.

RIE can be chosen as a solution to overcome the problems if

1. quick change is required.
2. requirements for existing resources are met.
3. problem solving in groups is needed or desired.
4. there is a desire to teach lean tools through direct application.
5. it is important to make people and organization think differently.

Pilot

Pilot is the implementation of lean on a small scale to test the solutions. For example, if a solution comes up to carry out an improvement in the management of pharmaceutical supplies and inpatient care in a hospital, the pilot can be carried out in only two inpatient rooms (Portioli-Staudacher, 2008).

The pilot results are used to make a decision whether revisions to the program need to be taken or if the program proves to be effective and can be applied on a broader scale. To find out whether the team is ready to conduct a pilot, the following checklist can be used.

Table 9.1   Pilot Checklist

Field of Work: _____		
Pilot Strategy	**Yes**	**No**
Has the pilot term been determined?		
Will the pilot be restricted to certain consumer segments?		
Will the pilot involve certain departments?		
Will the pilot involve a specific unit or application?		
Training Preparation	**Yes**	**No**
Have process participants been briefed and prepared?		
Have work paths or lines of the new process been planned?		
Have future condition maps been created and shared?		
Have new forms been created and shared?		
Have the new standard operating procedures been recorded and shared?		
Measurement Plan	**Yes**	**No**
Have the success indicators been agreed?		
Have checklist or other data collection methods been made?		
Have data collectors been trained and prepared?		
Adjustment Plan	**Yes**	**No**
Are feedback mechanisms available?		
Will there be any formal interview or focus group to collect experience data?		
Is there any plan for displaying pilot data?		
Is there any plan to accommodate adjustments to the solution?		

Multi-phase Implementation

Multi-phase implementation is a broader range of lean implementation programs, so it needs to be carried out in several stages. For example, multi-phase implementation activities to improve the electronic medical record system at the provincial to national level can take a minimum of five years (Trueman, 2009). Multi-phase implementation must be preceded by the pilot and sufficient data regarding the problem. For example, in the case of a multi-phase implementation to improve the start time of operating room, data collection on the factors that cause a delay in the start time of the operating room is carried out. Afterward, it is shown visually how the data collection runs well with the data obtained. Then, a three-phase implementation is performed to reduce the start time of the operating room (Darwish, Mehta, Mahmoud, El-sergany, & Culberson, 2016).

Poka Yoke

Fool proof, also called *poka yoke*, is a tool or method to reduce the possibility of making mistakes. The term *poka yoke* comes from Japanese which means to avoid (*yokeru*) mistakes (*poka*) (Dudek-Burlikowska & Szewieczek, 2009). Efforts to avoid the possibility of mistake are preventive steps that can increase productivity and please the consumers because there is no mistake in getting the services.

There are two types of *poka yoke*, which are hard *poka yoke* and soft *poka yoke*. Hard *poka yoke* is a design process that helps in avoiding mistakes and allowing preventive actions to be the part of design process. Soft *poka yoke* is an alarm signal that immediately detects a defect or error when it appears and gives a warning to the people there. Soft *poka yoke* can be applied in follow-up actions after FMEA (Failure Mode and Effect Analysis).

The types of error that can be addressed through *poka yoke* are human errors such as forgetting, misunderstanding, misidentification, knowing the mistake but repeating it anyway, good intentions that are not well implemented, lack of skills, intentional errors, unnecessary errors, slowness, lack of standards, surprise errors, and desired mistakes (Dudek-Burlikowska and Szewieczek, 2009). These mistakes are caused by factors such as lack of concentration, drawing conclusions too early, bad labels, insufficient training, rushing that ends up in taking shortcuts, not thinking, slow reaction or judgment, inconsistent methods, unexpected situations, and sabotage.

In line with the above explanation, the fool proofing process requires the following steps:

1. Identify errors or defects.
2. Determine the cause of errors.
3. Determine at what level the inspection can be carried out in the process.
4. Determine the suitable type of fool proofing.
5. Determine whether to take hard or soft *poka yoke*.
6. Design and implement *poka yoke*.
7. Test and improve methods.
8. Train the process participants.
9. Oversee the process for assessing effectiveness.
10. If a bad situation arises, work more to prevent errors at the source.

Pursuit of Perfection

Pursuit of perfection in lean context is intended to improve the process on an ongoing basis. Endless pursuit of perfection is the final part of lean philosophy (Jimmerson, Weber, & Sobek, 2005). It is a part of continuous improvement cycle. In this case, the concept of transfer of innovation and management of change is important.

Transfer of innovation is sharing any innovation that has been successfully applied in one department to another. Transfer of innovation is part of change management. General literature shows the factors of top leadership support to changes that are being made and communication about why changes are made and who are engaged (Sisson & Elshennawy, 2015), and all of them are very important for the success of change management and transfer of innovation.

In the context of health services, success in change management in health service organizations is determined by various factors such as the following (Thor, 2007):

1. Competition for needs of resources.
2. Access to knowledge, skills, experience, and other resources.
3. Participation of key stakeholders, conformity with the organizational situations, and compatibility of lean application.
4. Compatibility with organizational situations, capitalization of early success, and allocation of resources to maintain sustainability.
5. Success in presenting achievements, rewards, and performance.

DEVELOPING LEAN CULTURE

Chapter 10

Developing Lean Culture

After the situation is handled, lean culture should be developed, so that the goal to improve the situation on a continuous basis can be achieved. Culture, in the context of an organization, is

> a pattern of shared basic assumptions that have been learned when solving problems, which have worked well so that they can be considered as legitimate and hence, are being taught to new members as the proper way to see, think, and feel in relation to these problems.
>
> *(Morato, 2013)*

Based on this definition, lean culture is a culture in which lean is used when solving problems, is studied, and finally produces a pattern of basic assumptions of the members of an organization. In short, culture is the way people do things in an organization. In organizations with lean culture, people do their jobs based on lean principles and procedures (Mann, 2005). Organizations with lean culture have reaped many successful experiences in implementing lean, so it is seen as a legitimate basic assumption. New employees coming to an organization that applies lean culture will be taught to see, think, and feel from the lean perspective in dealing with problems in their jobs.

The effort to build a lean culture relies on the support and active participation of leaders as the agents of change. Research shows that the success of lean implementation is around 50% depending on leadership, while the remaining 30% is on finance, 10% on organization culture, and 10% on skills and expertise (Miina, 2012).

In general, leaders play a role in developing subordinates' problem-solving skills and producing various continuous improvement efforts. In addition, leaders are responsible for encouraging subordinates to continuously use problem-solving tools as part of their efforts to improve their subordinates' skills to deal with bigger problems.

There are also other roles of leaders at various organizational levels for successful lean implementation. Table 10.1 shows the various organizational roles and their contribution to maintain lean initiatives in an organization.

A leader is not a hero but rather a mentor for subordinates. A leader should believe that well-developed subordinates are not subordinates who know all the answers but subordinates who are able to know what the problem is. By knowing the problem, new answers can emerge through thinking processes that challenge old assumptions and weigh new possibilities.

Table 10.1 Roles of Leadership in Maintaining Lean

Organizational Level	Primary Contribution	Task	Secondary Contribution	Task
Strategic: senior (CEO, senior vice president)	Management; *steering* and *oversight*	Supporting cross-border perspective	Measurement; compliance to the process after project	Supervising cross-border indicators; Gemba
Programmatic: function (vice president, director)	Accountability	Fulfilling project commitment; managing cross border performance	Compliance is disciplined; commitment to the process after project	Cooperating in process management; Gemba
Tactical: department (manager, supervisor)	Tactical lean management system	Compliance is disciplined; Gemba	Colleagues involvement; continuous improvement	Educating, practicing problem solving from the root

Source: Mann (2009).

Besides the leader, there are other factors that are important for building a lean culture. Positive experience in running lean projects is another important factor that can build a lean culture since it creates enthusiasm and self-confidence that lean culture should be cultivated voluntarily and jointly within the company (Belhadi, 2017). In turn, it needs commitment from the employees. If the employees and leaders are committed, a clear strategy for creating a firm and sustainable lean culture is all the company needs (Al-Najem, 2014). To build this commitment, the role of lean teams is very important (Ballard & Rybkowksi, 2007). An effective lean team will be able to create successful lean implementation to develop the shared commitment to create a lean culture. In addition to the use of best practices from separated lean projects, lean culture is also built on an ongoing basis through iterative (Kaizen) continuous improvements. Kaizen is an effort to maintain the sustainability of the existing lean program, and it is a long-term continuous implementation. Maintaining consistency of Kaizen will enable lean culture to be built gradually in the organization by fostering employees' commitment (Kruskal, Reedy, Pascal, Rosen, & Boiselle, 2012).

From the above explanation, it can be concluded that lean culture is built by a number of factors, namely leadership, positive experience, employee commitment, clear strategy, and Kaizen. The interrelationship between these factors is shown in Figure 10.1.

From Figure 10.1, leadership is considered as the most determining factor for the success of lean culture. It is because leadership can drive the development of other factors. A good leader can gain success in lean implementation in a single way. A good leader is also able to encourage employee commitment. In addition, a good leader develops long-term strategies to achieve lean culture. For this reason, the discussion in this section will focus on the behavior of leaders which can create lean culture in the organization.

Figure 10.1   Driving factors of lean culture.

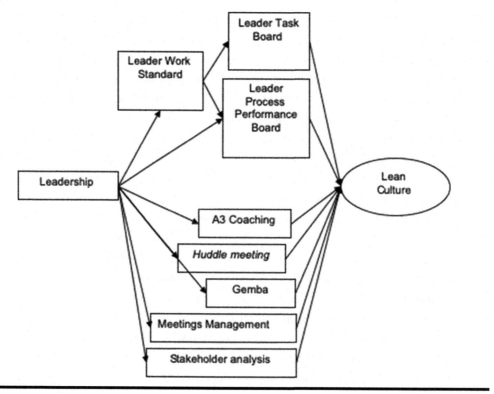

Figure 10.2 Framework for building a lean culture.

This chapter discusses a number of aspects of lean leadership. It starts with the standard work of lean leaders and important parts in the leader's visual management, which are the leader's task board and the leader's performance board. Furthermore, the techniques of the leader in managing lean culture are discussed such as A3 coaching, leader huddle meetings, leader process walk (Gemba), determination of the productivity of meetings, and stakeholder analysis.

Chapter 11

Leader Standard Work

Standard work, standardized work, and standard are three different things. The weakest situation is the standard situation, while standard work is the most satisfying situation. The difference between the three concepts is illustrated in Table 11.1.

Table 11.1   Differences between Standard, Standardized Work, and Standard Work

	Standard	*Standardized Work*	*Standard Work*
Level of Satisfaction	Low	Medium	High
Meaning	Target is the expected basic condition	Do it as planned; Basis to improvement	Proactive, taking action Analysis and improvement
Function	Support standardization Uniformity Determine normality (target)	Enable/support improvement Control, simplify, stabilize, routinize, and repeat Become an effective organization Achieve normality and knowing abnormalities	Process improvement action Development Become a learning organization Understand and take action on abnormalities
Main consideration	Expected performance	Current performance	Future performance

(Continued)

Table 11.1 (*Continued*)   Differences between Standard, Standardized Work, and Standard Work

	Standard	*Standardized Work*	*Standard Work*
Question	What are the targets?	Are the targets achieved? How to achieve targets?	Why are the targets not achieved? What is wrong? What is the solution?
Element	Measurement Tolerance Regulation/rules Procedure Characteristics	Work order or procedure Takt time calculation Supplies (stock, WIP (Work in Progress)) Layout planning	Operator/manager action If-then scenario, decision analysis, contingency Problem solving, solution to problems Adjustment to process/system
Format or tools	Specification Memo/notes Illustration Manual Figures Numbers	Standard operating procedure Instruction from operator Balance or improvement diagram Standard work process files Tracker diagram, task board Check list/audit	Tracker diagram, task board Resolution diagram Problem-resolution forms Analysis of root causes PDCA/Define, Measure, Analyze, Improve, Control (DMAIC) cycle Achievement board
Benefit	Remove variation Consistence of outcomes	Remove variation Efficient work Stable operation Flow optimization Consistence of outcomes	Preventive, remove variation Efficient decision-making Change the standardized work Stability, prevent flow collapse Improve process/system

Source: Hall (2013).

Figure 11.1   Lean as a closed loop system focused on the process (Mann, 2009).

Leader standard work comprises the daily activities of the leaders in a lean environment (Poksinska, Swartling, & Drotz, 2013). These daily activities include Gemba or reviewing the status of lean metrics. Leader standard work ensures that the standard processes at the lower and operational level run well while ensuring that the metrics are measured properly. If the metrics and standardization are guaranteed, then the problem solving and corrective actions can be performed well.

Furthermore, the leader standard work will ensure that the problem-solving process runs well and the resulting solution is executed properly (Mann, 2009). Mann (2009) sees that leader standard work is one of the three elements of lean management as a step to guide continuous improvement. In addition to leader standard work, other management elements are visual control and daily accountability. These are illustrated in Figure 11.1.

Appropriate tools need to be used and quick actions need to be taken by leaders to build lean culture in an organization. Tools and actions of leader standard work include the following:

1. Visual management

    For leaders, visual management aims to make the problem of the process clear at one look. Although information technology has been very helpful in carrying out work today, visual management is better done manually (by hand) compared to computer prints. There are many advantages of using a manual technique for visual management. Table 11.2 describes the benefits of manual visual management when compared to digital visual management.

    The following example shows a task board format for leadership actions. In this example, a simple structure task board is arranged using 3 × 5 paper/color cards. The index for this card is green to indicate the problem which has been resolved and red to indicate that resolution

Table 11.2 Differences between Visual Manual Management and Computer Management

Attribute	Manual	Information Technology
Information speed	Immediately at that moment	Slow since it is available after last data entry and at the latest time the data is implemented
Access of information	Immediately at the site; it is even understandable from 3 m away or more	Available to the person who access the computer
Accuracy of information	Not always accurate, sometimes vague, reporting period sometimes missed	Yes, absolutely, with the highest accuracy
Accurate information by verification	Can usually be seen directly since the location is near to the displayed visual	Accuracy often cannot be assessed; data is often far from the physical sources and reflects human opinion and data entry execution
Allow questions?	Yes, sometimes they can be asked and answered properly when the visual is displayed	Usually only questions which are designed in the report and which can be answered
Changeable and customable?	Yes, the form can be easily modified; new issues arise as new needs emerge	Rarely; often requires IT professionals or people with specific knowledge and experience to make changes, with the assumption that it does not conflict with other applications
Intimidation factor	Very low; as easy as coloring with crayons	May be intimidating to people who do not understand about the system
Ownership	Floor operators create permanent information in their area, often with their hand writings	Information is taken from the floor and changed into a computerized report without "fingerprints"
Information available simultaneously in many places?	No, except Kanban system with double cards	Absolutely, since it is an advantage of information technology

(Continued)

Table 11.2 (*Continued*) Differences between Visual Manual Management and Computer Management

Attribute	Manual	Information Technology
Accurate calculation?	Because it is manual, there is a possibility of error	Absolutely, since it is an advantage of information technology
Costs	Very low; use existing people with tools like pen and highlighter	Millions even billions since it involves tools, professionals, troubleshooting, consultants, etc.

Source: Mann (2005, p. 74).

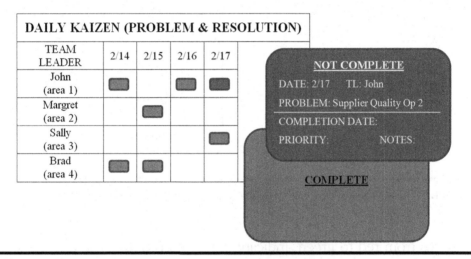

Figure 11.2 Example of leader visual management (Hall, 2013).

is still needed. Management verifies the status of problem solving by looking at data abnormalities based on time of appearance, team leader, and description of the problem (Figure 11.2).

At the beginning of each day, the leader can look at daily Kaizen task board. If there is no red card, the leader may continue the daily task. If there is a red card, the leader needs to gather necessary information. The leader then decides the priority and arranges the task. The leader chooses the highest-priority task. If there is more than one red card, the leader needs to seek for assistance from the management. The leader then chooses the team and identifies the problem through PDCA (Plan, Do, Check, and Act/Adjust) procedure. After this procedure is completed, the leader records the solution and changes the tag

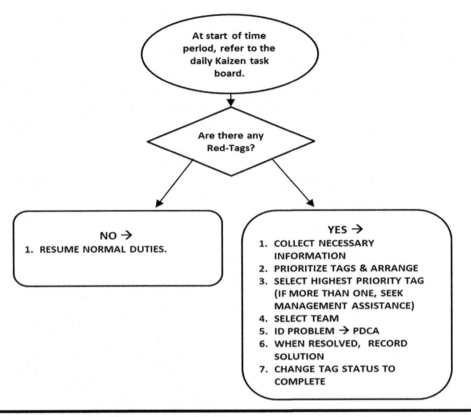

At start of time period, refer to the daily Kaizen task board.

Are there any Red-Tags?

NO →
1. RESUME NORMAL DUTIES.

YES →
1. COLLECT NECESSARY INFORMATION
2. PRIORITIZE TAGS & ARRANGE
3. SELECT HIGHEST PRIORITY TAG (IF MORE THAN ONE, SEEK MANAGEMENT ASSISTANCE)
4. SELECT TEAM
5. ID PROBLEM → PDCA
6. WHEN RESOLVED, RECORD SOLUTION
7. CHANGE TAG STATUS TO COMPLETE

Figure 11.3 Leader standard work for problem resolution (Hall, 2013).

status from red to green, indicating that the problem has been resolved. Figure 11.3 shows the flow of the problem-solving process.

Process performance board

Process performance board describes the process and flow of values needed for the leader and working group. With process performance board, the leader can monitor the situation periodically, for example, every 15 minutes. When abnormalities are found, the leader can make meeting with the operators to clarify the situation. The leader then documents the abnormal conditions on the problem form. If the problem is critical, the leader can contact management. If it is not critical, the leader can try to resolve the problem as soon as possible. If the problem can be resolved quickly, the leader can resolve the problem and fill in the problem form to be submitted to management. If the problem cannot be resolved immediately, the leader can fill the Kanban and place it on the task board. The leader then completes the task board assignment (Hall, 2013).

2. Leader process journey

Various health service professions are required to be able to identify opportunities to improve the quality of health services and thus increase the return on investment for health-care entrepreneurs. For example, EPAs (Entrustable Professional Activities) that must be complied by a geriatric specialist include periodically monitoring the system problems that can be improved by identifying deficiencies in patient care and improvement strategies (Leipzig et al., 2014). When there is a venous thromboembolism situation from the hospital, the hospital needs to establish a working group to review all thromboembolism incidents, assess the preventive practices by referring to evidence-based agency guidelines, and identify improvement opportunities for all patients in the hospital (Schleyer et al., 2016).

The general step taken to identify improvement opportunities is usually to hold a meeting with the people involved in the process (Middleton et al., 2009). Even so, meetings are not enough to audit and analyze compliance and identify opportunities for improvement. The leader and his team need to see the process that is happening in the field directly. The process journey is an effort to trace the process, monitor the process compliance, and identify opportunities for improvement.

3. Huddle meetings

Huddle meetings are daily team meetings to update status and progress. Huddle is carried out for 10–15 minutes, where the leader and unit staff focus on improving the process to identify current workflow weaknesses, create assignments, and build discipline throughout the day as a team (Barnas, 2011).

4. A3 problem solving

A3 problem solving aims to strengthen the problem-solving ability of the team. The problem-solving process is documented on A3 paper. This method was developed by Toyota Motor Corporation where a structured problem-solving approach is summarized on a piece of paper. The paper size is A3 or 11 in. × 17 in. The paper contains investigation, planning, and results of problem-solving or continuous improvement activities (Wiseman, 2011). In the previous chapter, we have presented an example of the A3 format. Figure 11.4 is another example of A3 format.

5. Coaching A3

Coaching is a significant part of on-the-job training. The leader guides the employees to help them develop problem-solving skills.

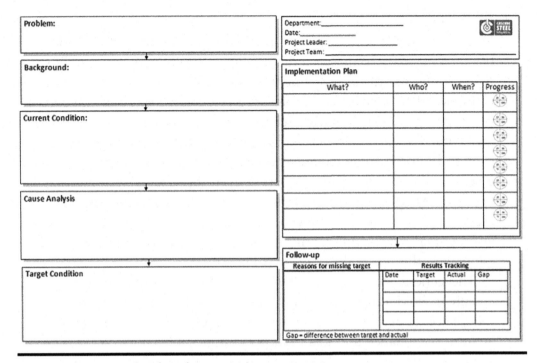

Figure 11.4 Example of A3 format (Wiseman, 2011).

> The leader needs to work with the coach or to be a coach or mentor for subordinates, if necessary, not only to build knowledge but also to build skills, including skills in problem solving (Wiseman, 2011).

The list above is not standard. In the case of ThedaCare, the lean team developed a number of leader standard tasks including the following (Barnas, 2011):

1. Prepare daily statistic file.
2. Manage daily huddle.
3. Build standard work which helps the leader to know what to do throughout the day.
4. Teach, guide, and become a mentor.
5. Collect data for monthly performance review meeting.
6. Develop a standard agenda for monthly performance review meetings.
7. Create and carry out activities to solve problems and communicate them.
8. Share problem information, report it, and if necessary, raise it to a higher level of organization.

Meanwhile, at Virginia Mason Hospital, leader standard work is divided into two: mandatory standard work for at least one leader and mandatory standard work for each leader (Lewis & Mann, 2014). Tables 11.3 and 11.4 contain standard work for each category along with the frequency of implementation.

Mann (2005, pp. 33–35) distinguishes standard types of work based on leaders who do it. There are three types of leaders, namely team leaders, supervisors, and value flow managers:

1. Team leader

    Team leaders' standard work is 80% more than their daily work since they have to be present in the field to monitor the process all the time. The remaining 20% of time is used to accommodate the variability of work because some standard work activities may require a longer time than usual. The team leaders' standard work includes many things from the beginning to the end of the production, regular monitoring, and maintenance of the production process. In addition, the standard work of team leaders also includes daily corrective work and periodic tasks such as training the operators.

Table 11.3 Leader Mandatory Standard Work Checklist for at Least One Leader

Checklist of Leader Standard Work	Frequency		
Mandatory Standard Work for at Least One Leader	Daily	Weekly	Monthly
Perform daily huddle with standard work	√		
Review and sign the Gemba production board (all day)	√		
Sweep the environment/work facilities	√		
Sweep the WIP (electronic system for urgent messages)	√		
Review Kronos (overtime, without breaks, etc.)	√		
Plan and schedule staff	√		
Conduct audit and safety check as required	√		
Review VMPS (Vision, Mission, Goal, Strategy) for leader status		√	
Track and analyze damage/problem trends of production board		√	
Update PeopleLink			

Source: Lewis and Mann (2014).

Table 11.4 Mandatory Standard Work Checklist for Each Leader

Checklist of Leader Standard Work	Frequency		
Mandatory Standard Work for Each Leader	Daily	Weekly	Monthly
Review variation in finance and reports (specific information/reports)	√		
Document and follow up problems	√		
Document and conduct follow-up RCA (root cause analysis) and defects	√		
Review and update the Kaizen plan	√		
Switch operations (leader transfer, service transfer, etc.)	√		
Perform Gemba observation supported by VMPS tools		√	
Applause		√	
Sweep the staff readiness: performance evaluation, Focus Group Discussion (FFD), etc.		√	
Review the Ganey Press			√

Source: Lewis and Mann (2014).

2. Supervisor

   The standard work of supervisors covers around 50% of their daily work. This standard work is mainly repeated daily or weekly. The standard work of a supervisor includes:

   a. Start the shifts and staffs.

   b. Review the previous production tracking document to understand and take further action needed to follow up on target or other issues that have not been achieved yet.

   c. Review the assignment of team leader that day and conduct a new assignment. It requires cooperation from the supervisors and team leaders as well as monitoring and verifying the implementation of team leaders' standard work.

3. Value flow manager

   The standard work of value flow managers covers 25% of their daily working hours, not to mention periodically scheduled off-field meetings. The standard work of value flow managers covers:

   a. Leading a daily brief, structured, accountability meeting as part of the daily accountability process.

b. Weekly Gemba trips with each supervisor to educate and check the homework.
c. Verification of the execution of supervisory standard work task.

An example of leader standard work implementation can be seen in the following ThedaCare case (Barnas, 2011). In this case, lean was directed to improve the performance of the surgical department at Appleton Medical Center. The unit manager and a group of leaders started the day by reviewing the statistical sheet to determine the risks on the quality and safety that occurred in the previous shift. They observed a knee infection in that unit. At 9:45 a.m., the daily huddle was carried out led by the manager, and all the staff members were present. The manager reported this infection and said there were four grade 1 knee infection cases in the last nine months at that unit. The manager then set two standard actions:

1. The manager asked the manager or supervisor to observe all knee surgeries to know the factors causing complications. It was to find ways to prevent other knee infections.
2. The manager created a working group, led by the unit supervisor, to develop an A3 sheet. The purpose was to find out the root problem of the knee infection incidence. This A3 sheet contained fishbone analysis and data from the doctor, time of the event, the operating room, and so on. The A3 preparation process was conducted for three months, where the progress was reported in the daily huddle. Meanwhile, the manager reported progress at the monthly performance meeting and included knee infection as an important part of safety/quality scorecard of the unit.

The team conducted interviews with doctors. The team found a doctor who never treated an infection case throughout his career. When they asked him what was different in his practice compared to that of other doctors, he answered that he used a different type of suture compared to other doctors. After carrying out this process, the group drew a conclusion that suture is a potential cause of knee infection problems. This suture was performed by two doctors. Based on this reason, the team developed a solution to replace the type of suture. Since then, there has never been a knee infection case. After six months, as there was no case of knee infection, knee infection was removed from the safety scorecard in the surgical unit.

Chapter 12

Leader Task Board

Leader task board is one of the leader standard works that reviews the statistics sheet, gives assignments, and monitors the process. It can only be conducted effectively if there are task boards. Task boards are very helpful to visualize the work so that it can be comprehensively reviewed. Without a clear picture, it is difficult to improve the ongoing process, and when improvement is needed, it will only be conducted locally due to limited description (Hajratwala, 2012). Aasland and Blankenburg (Aasland & Blankenburg, 2012b) refer to the task board as an information radiator, emphasizing the significance of information produced by the task board. A good task board must (Hajrawatha, 2012)

1. reflect the actual process in the field. It facilitates the observation of bottlenecks and hidden processes. Therefore, task board is better made by hand than by a computer program.
2. be easily modifiable in unexpected ways. This is why handwritten physical boards must be used. An easily modified work board is like a "living thing" which continues to grow and develop through the work done by the team (Aasland & Blankenburg, 2012a).
3. be rough. A neat and perfect board with standard writing and letters is boring, and people would tend to ignore the writing on the task board. It is because the writing is considered as a formality, has no important value, and is not personal. Handwritten board, which is readable will trigger creativity and problem solving.
4. be large and visible. The more visible, indeed, the more aware someone is of the importance of the writings, and hence, it will be easier to process it cognitively to make a conclusion and solution.

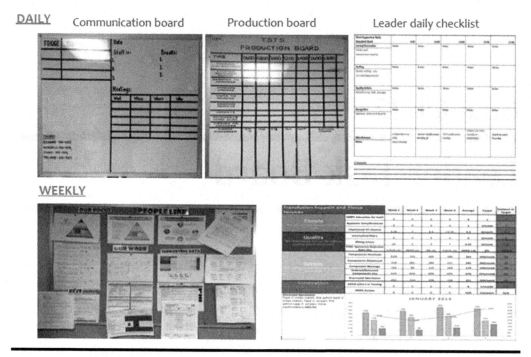

Figure 12.1 Examples of leader task board (Lewis & Mann, 2014).

Here are examples of five leader task boards reviewed by lean leaders at Virginia Mason Hospital. Three boards need to be reviewed every day, while the other two are reviewed every week. The boards daily reviewed are communication board, production board, and the leader's daily checklist. The boards reviewed weekly are PeopleLinks (various information) and performance board (Figure 12.1).

A3 Coaching

Referring to the example of the ThedaCare case, after the task board is created and used, the leader forms a team to prepare A3 regarding the problems they faced. A3 makes the problem-solving process transparent. Moreover, A3 is a good example to teach the employees how to solve problems within an organization, which eventually helps them to be active as problem solvers.

It should be kept in mind that A3 relies on PDCA process: Plan, Do, Check, and Act/Adjust. PDCA means that A3 approach gives space to determine the problem (Plan), fix the problem (Do), assess whether the problem has been resolved (Check), and refine the solution and correct it (Act/Adjust). The leader's job is to ask various questions that guide his subordinates to apply every element of PDCA. For example, at the Plan stage, you can ask: what they have learned from Gemba? What facts they have gathered to understand the current situation? What information they have revealed to confirm the hypothesis? What they have learned from the analysis? At the Do stage, questions can include the following: What does the patient think of the solution? Has A3 included input from the people involved? How can the proposed solution help solving the problem? What alternatives do the people think of to run the solution? At the Check and Adjust stage, the questions might be as follows: Has the team started to report problems and ideas? What is the capability of the team to learn from A3? What changes have they seen regarding staff who work on this issue? With whom have they shared A3 learning?

Materials of A3 coaching may include introduction and objectives, A3 report, background information, current condition, analysis of cause, measurement, identification of target condition, selection of target condition, implementation plan, and follow-up plan (Wiseman, 2011). Details of this curriculum include (Wiseman, 2011):

1. Introduction and objectives: introduction that can be raised, for example, the position of continuous improvement in the context of the quality system. The quality system can be analogous to an umbrella with continuous improvement as the handle. This umbrella covers things like product quality, customer satisfaction, A3 reports, and ISO certification (Figure 12.2).

Figure 12.2   Umbrella analogy (Wiseman, 2011).

The main objective is communicating process improvement activities using A3 report. The sub-objectives include the following:
a. Identify problems at work.
b. Analyze problems.
c. Determine and implement solutions to problems.
d. Measure the progress.
e. Identify additional changes needed.

2. A3 report

This section describes the history, concept, and format of an A3 report. The purpose of an A3 report is to document and manage continuous improvement activities such as documenting plans, decisions, and learning involved in problem solving and providing a structured problem-solving process. Another purpose of an A3 report is to facilitate communication in terms of developing a shared language to communicate continuous improvement. This section also explains the correlation between continuous improvement and PDCA.

3. Problem statement

It explains the first part of A3, namely the problem statement. Explanation about the meaning of a process and simple examples of the process are given to employees. Next is brainstorming, starting from the understanding and steps of brainstorming. The leader can directly invite participants to practice brainstorming to identify the processes requiring improvement in the workplace or problems that generally need to be corrected. The target of brainstorming is at least 10 ideas, and each idea is written on a sticky note. Participants are then given explanation about affinity diagram as a tool to manage ideas that emerge during brainstorming. Next, a practice session is conducted to develop an affinity diagram. Finally, participants are required to choose one problem as the main problem that must be solved together.

4. Background information

After the problem is identified, the participants explain the background of the problem. The background of the problem is part of A3 which covers information to describe the problem as a whole and clarify the significance of the problem for the organization. In this section, it is explained why this problem is important and needs to be solved by the organization. Participants are taught how to collect background information by, for example, identifying the stakeholders who can help understand the problem and creating a list of questions to be asked to the stakeholders.

5. Current condition

   The current condition is the next section of A3 after background information. The participants are asked to create a diagram that illustrates how the current process takes place. In this diagram, the problem that is previously targeted is highlighted.

6. First homework

   The participants are then given homework to be discussed in the next session. This homework includes the following:

   a. Identify problems that will be used for continuous improvement activities.

   b. Understand the problem deeper with at least two stakeholders.

   c. Collect background information.

   d. Document problems, background information, and current condition using process diagrams on an A3 report.

   e. Bring the A3 report to the next meeting.

7. Homework debrief

   In the following meeting, the learning begins with the review of the results of the homework. The participants share their A3 report in front of the class with other participants.

8. Cause analysis

   After each participant has an A3 report, the next learning is the cause analysis. The participants explain tools for root cause analysis such as Five Whys (5Ws), fishbone diagram, and Pareto diagram. The participants are also given examples of how to use these tools to solve problems. Figure 12.3 is an example of a fishbone diagram for the absence of standardization of biopsy specimens.

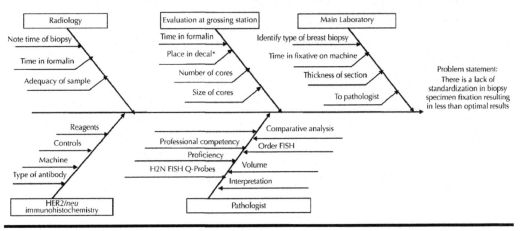

Figure 12.3 Example of fishbone diagram (Middleton et al., 2009).

9. Measurement

Measurement gives numerical data that provides an overview or feedback of the process performance. The participants are given explanation about the importance of measurement and the types of important measurements.

10. Identification of target condition

Identifying target conditions includes creating diagrams that illustrate how the proposed process can run better. In this section, there are changes that will address the roots of the identified problem. In addition, this section predicts the expected level of performance both descriptively and numerically.

11. Second homework

The participants are then given homework to be discussed in the next session. This homework includes the following:

a. Collect data and create a Pareto diagram and fishbone diagram for each problem.

b. Complete at least two 5Ws activities to identify potential root causes.

c. Add analysis results to the A3 report from previous homework.

d. Create three possible target conditions. These target conditions should not be included in the A3 report.

e. Decide which alternative the working group will be focused on and the reasons why this alternative is chosen.

f. Bring the updated A3 report to the next meeting.

12. Homework debrief

In the next meeting, the learning begins with a review of the results of the homework. The participants share their updated A3 report in front of the class with other participants. The participants also explain what difficulties they had when completing the work.

13. Selection of target condition

After debriefing, the selection of target condition from alternatives to existing target conditions is explained. Participants might be taught about the decision metric, which is a tool to compare various alternatives using criteria and weighting. After describing the benefits and steps, the participants are invited to create a decision metric. This practice consists of the following steps:

a. Submit three alternative target conditions that have been selected from the previous homework.

b. Identify at least four criteria that are assumed to be important.

c. Give a value to each criterion from 1 to 10.
d. Each alternative is then given a score (−1, 0, 1) for each criterion.
e. Calculate the total score of each alternative.
f. Make a decision about which alternatives need to be taken based on the total score obtained.
g. Reflect on whether this is different from what was suspected by the participants previously when making these alternatives at home.

The following is an example of a decision metric with seven alternatives relating to the shape of ideal hospital beds to replace old and damaged beds. In this example, there are seven alternative bed designs. The important criteria are production cost, development cost, maneuverability, safety, ease of installation, and configurability. The weight given to each criterion is 6 for production cost, 2 for development cost, 5 for maneuverability, 1 for safety, 3 for ease of installation, and 3 for configurability. Each alternative is then given a score as seen in Table 12.1. The total value is obtained by summing the results between values and weights. For example, the total value for the diagonal bed is $1 \times 6 + 1 \times 2 + 1 \times 5 + 1 \times 1 + 1 \times 3 + (−1) \times 3 = 6 + 2 + 5 + 1 + 3 − 3 = 14$.

Based on this example, the diagonal bed is chosen. This bed has the greatest total value compared to other alternative beds.

1. Implementation plan

     The participants are given an explanation on how to prepare an implementation plan. An implementation plan is prepared by making a list of actions that must be taken to achieve the target condition, who is responsible for the action, when is the deadline, and what is the progress of implementation process. Table 12.2 displays a template for making an implementation plan.

2. Follow-up plan

     It explains the measurable objectives for the performance of improvement process. The template in Table 12.3 shows the format for follow-up plan in A3 file. In this template, the gap concept is introduced. Gap is the difference between the target and the actual condition. First of all, the right column is filled with tracking results. The tracking results on the first date will identify the gap. This gap then explains why it could emerge and what solution to take can be filled in the left column.

Table 12.1 Example of Decision for Selecting Inpatient Bed Design Metric

Criteria/Alternative	Production Cost	Development Cost	Maneuverability	Safety	Ease of Installation	Configurability	Total
Weight	6	2	5	1	3	3	20
Diagonal	1	1	1	1	1	−1	14
Straight vertical	1	1	0	0	1	−1	8
Straight horizontal	1	1	0	0	1	−1	8
Three	0	1	1	1	0	−1	5
Four	−1	1	1	1	−1	−1	−4
Configurable	0	−1	1	1	0	1	7

Source: Qamar (2011).

3. Third homework

The participants are given homework as a close of the training. This homework includes the following:
a. Create process performance targets.
b. Submit actions to fill gaps.
c. Fill in this information in the follow-up section of A3 report.
d. Get permission from the head to implement the proposed changes.

Table 12.2   Implementation Plan Template

What?	Who?	When?	Progress
Action taken	Person in charge	Time and date	%

Source: Wiseman (2011).

Table 12.3   Follow-Up Plan Template

Reason for Unachieved Target and Corrective Steps	Tracking Result			
Reason why gap emerges Action taken for follow-up Notes on result	Date	Target	Actual	Gap

Source: Wiseman (2011).

Chapter 13

Leader Process Performance Board

Leader process performance board covers all aspects which comprise the responsibility of a leader. This performance board contains four elements which become continuous improvement targets in terms of the leader's responsibility, which are as follows:

1. HR, related to various aspects such as safety, human resource development, involvement, growth, and morale.
2. Quality, including effectiveness (accuracy and completeness) from the field of the responsibility of the leader.
3. Costs, including efficiency (capacity and savings) from the field of the responsibility of the leader.
4. Delivery, including commitment to deliver output from the products of the field under leader's responsibility. The metrics used are quantity and time.

Performance board for each aspect contains the components of title, objectives, current achievement, trend, baseline, and a number of simple graphs. All of these components are spread over four PDCA lines. It means that HR has its own PDCA, quality has its own PDCA, and so on. The HR aspect can be broken down into more detailed aspects related to HR such as work and safety, depending on their relevance to the field that becomes the responsibility of the leader.

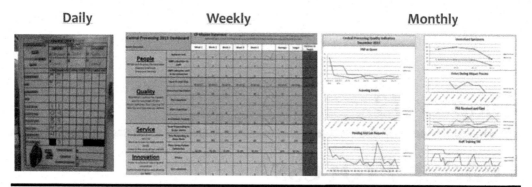

Figure 13.1 Examples of leader process performance board.

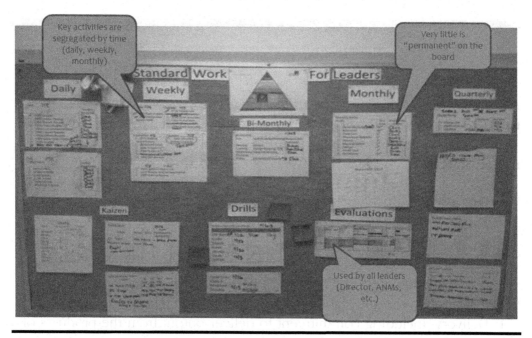

Figure 13.2 Example of composite process performance board (Lewis & Mann, 2014).

Figure 13.1 shows examples of daily, weekly, and monthly process performance boards. It can be seen that the daily board is manual and can be updated immediately. Weekly board is in a printed form documenting daily board results to avoid data loss and also summarize other data. Monthly board is in the form of a graphic displaying overall development trends.

Figure 13.2 shows an example of a complete process performance board containing daily, weekly, and monthly data. On this board, key activities are segregated based on time (i.e., daily, weekly, monthly). Only a few of

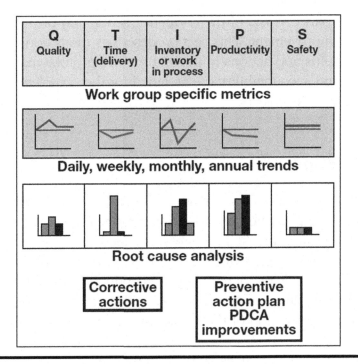

Figure 13.3   Example of QTIPS performance board.

the permanent data are stored on this board. This board can be used by all types of leaders including the director and manager.

Figure 13.3 shows another example of a process performance board using the QTIPS (Quality, Time, Inventory, Productivity, and Safety) indicator. This board consists of four parts. The upper part consists of five boxes, each of which is a part of each QTIPS indicator. These boxes contain tables of all days in a month. The performance column is filled every day with red and green codes. Red code means the metric has failed, while green code means the metric has been successfully achieved.

The second part is the trend chart from the above metric. This chart reflects daily, weekly, monthly, and yearly trends. This chart is in red, blue, and green codes. Red means *fail*. Blue means the edge between success and failure. Green indicates the time when the metric reaches the target.

The third part is the analysis part of the root cause. It only highlights the aspects that failed to reach the second part target. It uses various analyses such as Pareto graphic and root cause analysis. It answers the surrounding aspects of problem such as what, when, why, and how. Note that there is no question about who, to prevent the focus distracted to the person in charge rather than the problem itself.

The bottom part consists of the corrective action and preventive plan as well as PDCA improvement. This section describes the actions taken to overcome the problems and actions to prevent recurring problems. In addition, responsibility and accountability are assigned for the completion of the plan. It also has A3-PDCA projects.

Huddle Meetings

In the ThedaCare case, it is also mentioned that there is a huddle meeting. Huddle meeting is an ad hoc meeting to rearrange situational awareness, strengthen the existing plans, and assess the need to adjust the plan to actual situations (Edbrooke-Childs et al., 2018). Furthermore, the concept of situational awareness is defined as "the perception of elements in the environment within a volume of time and space, the comprehension of their meaning and the projection of their status in the near future" (Edbrooke-Childs et al., 2018).

In the field of health services, we can draw examples of how huddle meetings are used continuously in SAFE (Situation Awareness for Everyone) project. SAFE is a project to redirect the view of the clinical team on patients and diseases. This concept is called as clinical gaze (Lachman, 2013). SAFE is conducted for three years. The clinical team conducts a periodic huddle meeting. In fact, this is the main intervention in the SAFE program. It is because huddle creates a situational awareness, and this situational awareness raises the awareness of risks in real time in inpatient facilities, so that steps can be taken to reduce the safety risks.

In a huddle meeting, many issues such as various risk indicators or decays, staff attention, and various clinical indicators are discussed. Lean tools are also utilized to do this task. It is known that a huddle meeting in the SAFE case can increase situation awareness and bring opportunities to determine what actions can be taken to mitigate the risks and prevent the deterioration of patient health (Brady et al., 2013).

Research shows that huddle meetings have a positive effect on increasing the efficiency of staff members, improving accountability, improving cooperation culture and sense of togetherness, improving the quality of information sharing processes, and raising empowering feelings in participants. This overall improves the quality of awareness of participants in huddle meetings on existing problems and facilitates the capacity of participants to solve these problems (Goldenhar, Brady, Sutcliffe, & Muething, 2013).

The main task of huddle meetings is to identify problems, develop a shared understanding of the problem, and make plans to mitigate the problem. The main foundation of huddle meetings is the theory of change, stating that huddle allows efficient and collaborative information exchange in team work which in turn creates a shared view of the situation that occurs (Brady et al., 2013). In the health sector, this is proved by a research showing that increasing awareness of the situation can reduce 50% of patient transfers to higher levels of unplanned care (Brady et al., 2013).

Ideally, a huddle meeting is conducted for 10–15 minutes, led by leaders, and aims at optimizing staff involvement and focusing on basic information only (Edbrooke-Childs et al., 2018). Therefore, the quality of a huddle meeting is assessed from the following (Edbrooke-Childs et al., 2018):

1. Clear structure in the meeting.
2. No distraction or external interruption.
3. Everyone having an opportunity to contribute and consideration of all points of view.
4. Opportunity to identify potential problems and discuss the concrete plan to mitigate the problem.

Chapter 14

Leader Process Walk

We have discussed earlier about Gemba or process walk to collect the data to develop a map of the current process (Malpass, 2017). Gemba is carried out every day, and it covers various metrics which form the basis of leader standard work. These metrics are summarized as QTIPS (Quality, Time, Inventory, Productivity, and Safety) (Zarbo et al., 2015). Examples of metrics from each category of laboratory case in a hospital are presented in Table 14.1 (Zarbo et al., 2015).

These metrics should meet these requirements (Zarbo et al., 2015):

1. Metrics must focus on the customer. In a hospital setting, it means focusing on patient care and reflection of values in a unit.
2. Metrics must be simple, and collecting and comparing them must not take much time.
3. Metrics must reflect the stability (instability) of the process within the last 24 hours.
4. Metrics must be measured objectively and must not be vulnerable to personal bias or subjectivity.

Leaders are no exception; they must also take part in this activity. Leaders must perform the process walk because they are the ones who are most likely to get an overall picture of the process and access to the process. Moreover, it will build a culture because it provides a model for the subordinates about how to do a process walk. In the process walk, many things that are not revealed by the testimony of the people in the meeting can be found. For example, leaders may find that a number of nurses do not wash

Table 14.1 Examples of Metrics for Daily Management in Laboratory

Laboratory	Domain	Metric	Target Condition
Clinical chemistry	Quality	Modification to previously released results	0 mistake/day
	Time	Turnaround time to troponin I cardiac from ICU	90% results are reported within 30 minutes after prescription is accepted
	Safety	Fault in critical value notification (including documentation)	0 mistake/day
Transfusion medicine	Inventory	Availability of O-negative unit	> 50 units must be available
Microbiology serology	Quality	Outlier of PCR (Polymerase Chain Reaction)	0 control mistake/day
	Time	Turnaround time to RPR (Rapid Plasma Reagin)	100% reported at 10 a.m. the following day
	Productivity	Instrument (Vitek, bioMerieux, Durham, NC) downtime	No instrument downtime
Lab service center	Productivity	Waiting time of service center<60 seconds	> 80% calls are answered within 60 seconds
Lab support	Quality	Settlement of order from lab client of particular coverage	0 mistake/day
Coagulation	Quality	Modification to previously reported results	0 mistake/day
	Time	Turnaround time to PT/PTT/INR (Prothrombin Time/Partial Thromboplastin Time/International Normalized Ratio) from ICU	90% results are reported within 30 minutes after specimen is accepted
	Inventory	Instrument (Stago, Diagnostica Stago, Parsippany, NJ) downtime	No instrument downtime

(Continued)

Table 14.1 (*Continued*)   Examples of Metrics for Daily Management in Laboratory

Laboratory	Domain	Metric	Target Condition
	Safety	Fault in critical value notification (including documentation)	0 mistake/day
Hematology	Quality	Modification to previously reported results	0 mistake/day
	Time	Turnaround time to CBC (Complete Blood Count) from ICU	90% results are reported within 30 minutes after specimen is accepted
	Inventory	Differential count pending transferred between shifts	None; all differentials are reported in the same shift
	Safety	Fault in critical value notification (including documentation)	0 mistake/day
Core lab manual fluids	Inventory	Pending vaginosis screening	None; all screenings are reported in the same shift
Urinalysis	Quality	Modification to previously reported results	0 mistake/day
	Time	Turnaround time to urinalysis from ICU	90% results are reported within 30 minutes after specimen is accepted
	Inventory	Instrument downtime	No instrument downtime
Outreach	Safety	Call back of stats test result	100% stats test results are informed within 4 hours after the specimen collection call

(*Continued*)

Table 14.1 (*Continued*)   Examples of Metrics for Daily Management in Laboratory

Laboratory	Domain	Metric	Target Condition
Surgical pathology	Quality	Standard batch for regular block	0 mistake/day
	Time	Time spent to identify a mistake related to order in EMR (Electronic Medical Record)	0 mistake/day
	Inventory	Pending block transferred between shifts	None; all blocks must be processed in the same shift
	Safety	Specimen identification error	0 mistake/day
Cytopathology	Quality	Complaints related to order and HPV (Human Papillomavirus) results	0 mistake/day
	Time	Turnaround time of gynecology cases	100% received within 5 days
	Safety	Weekly 5S compliance (workplace organization)	100% compliance
Molecular pathology	Quality	Double EMR order	0 mistake/day
	Productivity	Pathologist does not include LIS (*Laboratory Information System*) order	0 mistake/day

Source: Zarbo et al. (2015).

their hands when they enter patient room and some nurses do not wash their hands when they leave the patient room (Williams, Fritz, Lovejoy, & Ed, 2014). This fact may not be reported by the nurses since they are afraid that they will be considered undisciplined or because they do not see the overall overview. Moreover, the nurse leader can directly ask the nurses why they did not wash their hands when they were caught not washing their hands.

Productivity of Meetings

The effectiveness of a meeting is determined by a number of aspects (Mieczakowski, Goodman-deane, Patmore, & Clarkson, 2014):

1. Broader project and organizational management. A thorough preparation behind the scenes is needed before the meeting is conducted by moderators, individuals, and groups, in order to create a coherent and productive meeting (Ding et al., 2007). Meeting schedules and management are also important. A good meeting is a periodic but brief one (Powell, Piccoli, & Ives, 2004).

2. Characteristics of participants and team. Group cohesion is very important for the success of a meeting (Ehsan, Mirza, & Ahmad, 2008). A team with similar background (Olson & Olson, 2000) and has a strong social bound can hold the meeting more effectively. If the meeting participants lack in group cohesion, give more time for their socialization (Prasad & Akhilesh, 2002) or have a group formation activity and face-to-face meeting before the actual meeting (Powell et al., 2004).

3. Meeting facilitation. Preparation involves audio video technology, props, lighting, logistics, agenda, supply, and so on.

4. Participant behavior during meeting. Individual behavior of the participants during the meeting can affect the effectiveness of the meeting. Good meeting behavior is to introduce yourself before speaking. Participants who do not behave well during the meeting may cause problems to other participants (Yankelovich et al., 2004). Participants who are distracted, for example, doing other things during the meeting, will distract other participants also. So, it will be difficult for them to remember and recall the information and what happened during the meeting (Edwards & Gronlund, 1998). There should be clear rules on how the meeting should run, and these rules are made before or at the beginning of the meeting.

The stages in an effective meeting follow the DEEPAND framework (Garcia, Kunz, & Fischer, 2003). DEEPAND stands for Description, Explanation, Evaluation, Prediction, Alternative formulation, Negotiation, and Decision-making (Khanzode, Fischer, Reed, & Ballard, 2006). DEEPAND means that a meeting is initiated with a description of the problem (if it is a follow-up meeting, problem means the achievement of the team since the previous meeting), explaining the problem, evaluating the problem, predicting what happens if the problem continues, finding solutions to problems, negotiation regarding solutions and responsibilities of the people to selected solutions, and making decisions about implementing solutions. In addition, at the end of the session, it is necessary to schedule the next meeting and the

Table 14.2   Example of RACI Metric

	Member 1	Member 2	Member 3	Member 4	Member 5	Member 6
Task 1	C	C,I				R,A
Task 2	A		C,I		R	
Task 3			A	R		I
Task 4	R	C			A	
Task 5			R	A		
Task 6	A	R			C	

Source: Vaanila (2015).

agenda to be discussed at the meeting and review the strengths (pluses) and weaknesses that must be corrected (delta) from the meeting.

In the meeting, a review of RACI metric may also be conducted. RACI stands for Responsible, Accountable, Consulted, and Informed. Firstly, the tasks to be carried out are submitted. Then, the names or roles needed in the task are listed. Next, a metric is created with columns containing roles and rows of tasks. Each relevant cell is named R, A, C, or I, with the following rules (Kozina & Sekovanic, 2015):

R=Responsible, i.e., people who are operationally responsible for task performance. One task may consist of several R's. An activity without R means that the activity cannot be completed.

A=Accountable, i.e., people who are personally responsible for and give the final approval. Every activity must have one A, no less, no more. A can be the same person as R.

C=Consulted, i.e., people who provide support in providing reviews, tips, and explanations. C is consulted before the project.

I=Informed, i.e., people who receive the report on the progress of the project. I receives the report after project.

Table 14.2 is an example of RACI metric.

Stakeholder Analysis

Another important task for a leader is to carry out stakeholder analysis. Stakeholders are those who influence and/or are influenced by an intervention or program. Stakeholders are organizations and individuals involved in

Table 14.3   Stakeholders in Medicine Preparation

Stakeholder	Interest
Head of the department	Brief introduction to new drugs Keeping the drug available Avoiding overload and sudden orders Having an aggregation of inventory management information
Unit manager	Having accurate data about costs and service delivery
Planner	Reliable production forecasting Avoiding overload and sudden orders Accurate and reliable inventory data
Pharmacist	Ability to fulfill customer demand Flexible production Production process without mistakes Producing high quality medicine

Source: de Vries (2011).

certain activities as stakeholders are organizations and individuals involved in certain activities because they participate in producing, consuming, managing, regulating, or evaluating the activities (Hyder et al., 2010). Table 14.3 is a list of key stakeholders in an inventory system of health services (De Vries, 2011).

There are many methods of stakeholder analysis in the literature (Hyder et al., 2010). One of the commonly used methods is identifying stakeholders and then determining their relationship with the project (as an authority, party who influences the results, or party to be influenced), determining the position of attitude (refusal, neutral, support), determining what is needed from these parties (e.g., HR, data, solution, implementation), and developing strategies to influence them.

References

Aasland, K., & Blankenburg, D. (2012a). An Analysis of the Uses and Properties of the Obeya. *18th International Conference on Engineering, Technology and Innovation, ICE 2012- Conference Proceedings*, (April 2017). https://doi.org/10.1109/ICE.2012.6297660.

Aasland, K., & Blankenburg, D. (2012b). Virtualizing the Obeya. In *NordDesign 2012*. Aalborg.

Adnan, A. N. B., Jaffar, A. B., Yusoff, N. B., & Halim, N. H. B. A. (2013). Implementation of just in time production through kanban system. *Industrial Engineering Letters, 3*(6), 11–20. Retrieved from http://www.iiste.org/Journals/index.php/IEL/article/view/6228%5Cnhttp://www.iiste.org/Journals/index.php/IEL/article/download/6228/6357.

Aghlmand, S., Lameei, A., & Small, R. (2010). A hands-on experience of the voice of customer analysis in maternity care from Iran. *International Journal of Health Care Quality Assurance, 23*(2), 153–170. https://doi.org/10.1108/09526861011017085.

Ahmad, M. O., Markkula, J., & Oivo, M. (2013). Kanban in software development: A systematic literature review. In *Software Engineering and Advanced Applications (SEAA)*, (pp. 9–16). IEEE. https://doi.org/10.1109/SEAA.2013.28

Al-najem, M. (2014). *Investigating the Factors Affecting Readiness for Lean System Adoption within Kuwaiti Small and Medium- Sized Manufacturing Industries*.

AllAboutLean. (2015). The (True) Difference Between Push and Pull What It Is Not! – Common Misconceptions. Retrieved on April 1, 2019, from https://www.allaboutlean.com/push-pull/.

Arnheiter, E. D., & Maleyeff, J. (2005). The integration of lean management and Six Sigma. *The TQM Magazine, 17*(1), 5–18. https://doi.org/10.1108/09544780510573020.

Austin, E. A. (2015). *Family-Centered Pediatric Radiation Therapy : A Nurse-Led Quality Improvement Collaboration Model*. California State University.

Bahensky, J. A, Roe, J., & Bolton, R. (2005). Lean sigma–will it work for healthcare? *Journal of Healthcare Information Management : JHIM, 19*(1), 39–44. Retrieved from http://citeseerx.ist.psu.edu/viewdoc/download?doi=10.1.1.127.4549&rep=repl&type=pdf%5Cnhttp://www.ncbi.nlm.nih.gov/pubmed/15682675.

Ballard, G., & Rybkowksi, Z. (2007). *The Evidence-Based Design Literature Review and Its Potential Implications for Capital Budgeting of Healthcare Facilities.*

Barandika, G., Beitia, J., Ruiz-de-Larramendi, I., & Fidalgo, M.-L. (2013). EFQM-Based PDCA Cycle Applied on Self-Learning Material for Chemistry Students. In *Edulearn13: 5th International Conference on Education and New Learning Technologies,* Barcelona, Spain, 1–3 July (pp. 5033–5038).

Barnas, K. (2011). ThedaCare's business performance system: Sustaining continuous daily improvement through hospital management in a lean environment. *The Joint Commission Journal on Quality and Patient Safety, 37*(9), 387–399.

Bassuk, J. A., & Washington, I. M. (2013). The a3 problem solving report: A 10-step scientific method to execute performance improvements in an academic research vivarium. *PloS One, 8*(10), 1–9. https://doi.org/10.1371/journal.pone.0076833.

Belhadi, A. (2017). Lean Deployment in SMEs, Performance Improvement and Success Factors : A Case Study (pp. 928–945).

Ben-Tovim, D. I., Bassham, J. E., Bennett, D. M., Dougherty, M. L., Martin, M. A., O'Neill, S. J., … Szwarcbord, M. G. (2008). Redesigning care at the flinders medical centre: Clinical process redesign using "lean thinking". *The Medical Journal of Australia, 188*(6 Suppl), 27–31. https://doi.org/ben11046_fm [pii].

Bengtsson, S., & Sjoblom, T. (2006). *A Flow Cost Model - A Case Study at Volvo Trucks Corporation.* Lulea University of Technology.

Bevilacqua, M., Ciarapica, F. E., De Sanctis, I., Mazzuto, G., & Paciarotti, C. (2015). A Changeover Time Reduction through an integration of lean practices: A case study from pharmaceutical sector. *Assembly Automation, 35*(1), 22–34. https://doi.org/10.1108/AA-05-2014–035.

Beynon-Davies, P., & Lederman, R. (2017). The management of operations making sense of visual management through affordance theory. *Production Planning & Control, 7287,* 1–16. https://doi.org/10.1080/09537287.2016.1243267.

Bortolotti, T. (2010). *Achieving Multiple - Performance Excellence Through Lean Manufacturing : Empirical Evidences Using Cumulative and Trade-off Models.* University of Bergamo.

Bracket Smack Down. (2019). Work in Process vs Work in Progress. Retrieved on April 1, 2019, from https://bracketsmackdown.com/work- in-process-vs-work-in-progress.html.

Brady, P. W., Muething, S., Kotagal, U., Ashby, M., Gallagher, R., Hall, D., … Wheeler, D. S. (2013). Improving situation awareness to reduce unrecognized clinical deterioration and serious safety events. *Pediatrics, 131*(1), e298–e308. https://doi.org/10.1542/peds.2012-1364.

Braganca, S., & Costa, E. (2015). An application of the lean production tool standard work. *Jurnal Teknologi, 76*(1), 47–53.

Bwemelo, G. S. (2016). Improving public service delivery in tanzania through kaizen: A review of empirical evidence. *Business Education Journal, I*(2), 1–21.

Card, A. J. (2017). The problem with "5 whys." *BMJ Quality and Safety, 26*(8), 671–677. https://doi.org/10.1136/bmjqs–2016–005849.

Celano, G., Costa, A., Fichera, S., & Tringali, G. (2012). Linking Six Sigma to simulation: A new roadmap to improve the quality of patient care. *International Journal of Health Care Quality Assurance*, *25*(4), 254–273. https://doi.org/10.1108/09526861211221473.

Chang, C.-M. (2007). *Integrating Lean and Six Sigma Methodologies for Service Quality Improvement and Innovative Design*. National Chiao Tung University.

Chang, H. (2015). Evaluation framework for telemedicine using the logical framework approach and a fishbone diagram. *Healthcare Informatics Research*, *21*(4), 230–238.

Cox, P. (2002). *Improving Learning Processes: Principles, Strategies and Techniques*. London.

Darwish, A., Mehta, P., Mahmoud, A., El-sergany, A., & Culberson, D. (2016). Improving operating room start times in a community teaching hospital. *Journal of Hospital Administration*, *5*(3), 1–7. https://doi.org/10.5430/jha.v5n3p33.

de Koning, H., Verver, J. P., van den Heuvel, J., Bisgaard, S., & Does, R. J. M. (2005). Lean Six Sigma in healthcare. *Journal of Healthcare Quality*, *28*, 4–11. https://doi.org/10.1111/j.1945-1474.2006.tb00596.x.

De Vries, J. (2011). The shaping of inventory systems in health services: A stakeholder analysis. *International Journal of Production Economics*, *133*(1), 60–69. https://doi.org/10.1016/j.ijpe.2009.10.029.

Dickson, E. W., Anguelov, Z., Vetterick, D., Eller, A., & Singh, S. (2009). Use of lean in the emergency department: A case series of 4 hospitals. *Annals of Emergency Medicine*, *54*(4), 504–510. https://doi.org/10.1016/j.annemergmed.2009.03.024.

Dickson, E. W., Singh, S., Cheung, D. S., Wyatt, C. C., & Nugent, A. S. (2009). Application of lean manufacturing techniques in the emergency department. *Journal of Emergency Medicine*, *37*(2), 177–182. https://doi.org/10.1016/j.jemermed.2007.11.108.

Ding, X., Erickson, T., Kellogg, W. A., Levy, S., Christensen, J. E., Sussman, J., … Bennett, W. E. (2007). An Empirical Study of the Use of Visually Enhanced VoIP Audio Conferencing: The Case of IEAC. In *Proceedings of the SIGCHI Conference on Human Factors in Computing Systems (CHI '07)* (p. 1019). https://doi.org/10.1145/1240624.1240780.

Dudek-Burlikowska, M., & Szewieczek, D. (2009). The Poka-Yoke method as an improving quality tool of operations in the process. *Journal of Achievements in Materials and Manufacturing Engineering*, *36*(1), 95–102.

Edbrooke-Childs, J., Hayes, J., Sharples, E., Gondek, D., Stapley, E., Sevdalis, N., … Deighton, J. (2018). Development of the huddle observation tool for structured case management discussions to improve situation awareness on inpatient clinical wards. *BMJ Quality & Safety*, *27*, 365–372. https://doi.org/10.1136/bmjqs–2017–006513.

Edwards, M. B., & Gronlund, S. D. (1998). Task interruption and its effects on memory. *Memory*, *6*(6), 665–687. https://doi.org/10.1080/741943375.

Ehsan, N., Mirza, E., & Ahmad, M. (2008). Impact of Computer-Mediated Communication on Virtual Teams' Performance: An Empirical Study. In *2008 International Symposium on Information Technology* (Vol. 2, pp. 1–8). https://doi.org/10.1109/ITSIM.2008.4632068.

Feng, P. P., & Tommelein, I. D. (2009). *Causes of Rework in California Hospital Design and Permitting: Augmenting Existing Taxonomy. In Proceedings of IGLC17: 17th Annual Conference of the International Group for Lean Construction* (pp. 407–416). Pingtung, Taiwan: National Pingtung University of Science and Technology.

Fernandes, N. O., & Carmo-Silva, S. (2009). How to release orders with sequence-dependent setup times? In *Proceedings of the World Congress on Engineering 2009* (Vol. I, pp. 3–6). London.

Ferradás, P. G., & Salonitis, K. (2013). Improving changeover time: A tailored SMED approach for welding cells. *Procedia CIRP, 7,* 598–603. https://doi.org/10.1016/j.procir.2013.06.039.

Fillingham, D. (2007). Can lean save lives? *Leadership in Health Services, 20*(4), 231–241. https://doi.org/10.1108/17511870710829346.

Fine, B. A., Golden, B., Hannam, R., & Morra, D. (2009). Leading lean: A Canadian healthcare leader's guide. *Healthcare Quarterly, 12*(3), 32–41.

Frøvold, K., Muller, G., & Pennotti, M. (2017). Applying A3 Reports for Early Validation and Optimization of Stakeholder Communication in Development Projects. In *27th Annual INCOSE International Symposium,* Adelaide Convention Centre, North Terrace – Adelaide, South Australia 5000 – Australia, Saturday, July 15 – Thursday, July 20.

Garcia, A. C. B., Kunz, J., & Fischer, M. (2003). *Meeting Details: Methods to Instrument Meetings and Use Agenda Voting to Make Them More Effective* (No. 147). https://doi.org/10.1016/S0168-0102(05)00140-9.

Giacchetta, G., & Marchetti, B. (2013). Medical waste management: a case study in a small size hospital of central Italy. *Strategic Outsourcing: An International Journal, 6*(1), 65–84. https://doi.org/10.1108/17538291311316072

Goldenhar, L. M., Brady, P. W., Sutcliffe, K. M., & Muething, S. E. (2013). Huddling for high reliability and situation awareness. *BMJ Quality and Safety, 22*(11), 899–906. https://doi.org/10.1136/bmjqs-2012-001467.

Guimaraes, C. M., & de Carvalho, J. C. (2013). Strategic outsourcing: A lean tool of healthcare supply chain management. *Strategic Outsourcing: An International Journal, 6*(2), 138–166. https://doi.org/10.1108/SO-11-2011-0035.

Gunasekaran, A., Mcneil, R., McGaughey, R., & Ajasa, T. (2001). Experiences of a small to medium size enterprise in the design and implementation of manufacturing cells. *International Journal of Computer Integrated Manufacturing, 14*(2), 212–223. https://doi.org/10.1080/09511920150216332.

Hajratwala, N. (2012). Task Board Evolution. In *Proceedings – 2012 Agile Conference, Agile 2012* (pp. 111–116). https://doi.org/10.1109/Agile.2012.32.

Hall, K. W. (2013). Process improvement through established standard work. *Technology Interface International Journal, 13*(2), 20–30.

Hallam, C. R. A., & Contreras, C. (2016). The Interrelation of Lean and Green Manufacturing Practices: A Case of Push or Pull in Implementation. In *2016 Proceedings of PICMET '16: Technology Management for Social Innovation*, Waikiki Beach Marriott Resort & Spa, Honolulu, Hawaii, USA, pp. 1815–1823.

Haneyah, S., Hurink, J., Schutten, M., Zijm, H., & Schuur, P. (2011). *Planning and Control of Automated Material Handling Systems : The Merge Module*.

Holden, R. J. (2011). Lean thinking in emergency departments: A critical review. *Annals of Emergency Medicine, 57*(3), 265–278. https://doi.org/10.1016/j.annemergmed.2010.08.001.

Holweg, M. (2007). The genealogy of lean production. *Journal of Operations Management, 25*, 420–437. https://doi.org/10.1016/j.jom.2006.04.001.

Hopp, W. J., & Van Oyen, M. P. (2003). Agile workforce evaluation: A framework for cross-training and coordination. *IIE Transactions, 36*, 1–32.

Hyder, A., Syed, S., Puvanachandra, P., Bloom, G., Sundaram, S., Mahmood, S., … Peters, D. (2010). Stakeholder analysis for health research: Case studies from low- and middle-income countries. *Public Health, 124*(3), 159–166. https://doi.org/10.1016/j.puhe.2009.12.006.

Ikonen, M. (2011). *Lean Thinking in Software Development : Impacts of Kanban on Projects*. University of Helsinki.

Jagim, M. K. (2013). *Development of the Jagim Lean Real Time Location Systems Model for Healthcare*. North Dakota State University.

Jimmerson, C., Weber, D., & Sobek, D. K. (2005). Reducing waste and errors: Piloting lean principles at intermountain healthcare. *Joint Commission Journal on Quality and Patient Safety, 31*(5), 249–257. https://doi.org/10.1016/S1553-7250(05)31032-4.

Jones, C., Medlen, N., Merlo, C., Robertson, M., & Shepherdson, J. (2000). The lean enterprise. *BT Technology Journal, 17*, 15–22.

Kanamori, S., Sow, S., Castro, M. C., Matsuno, R., Tsuru, A., & Jimba, M. (2015). Implementation of 5S management method for lean healthcare at a health center in Senegal: A qualitative study of staff perception. *Global Health Action, 8*(1), 27256. https://doi.org/10.3402/gha.v8.27256.

Khanzode, A., Fischer, M., Reed, D., & Ballard, G. (2006). *A Guide to Applying the Principles of Virtual Design & Construction (VDC) to the Lean Project Delivery Process. CIFE Working Paper #093*. Retrieved from http://www.stanford.edu/group/CIFE/online.publications/WP093.pdf.

Kim, C. S., Spahlinger, D. A., Kin, J. M., & Billi, J. E. (2006). Lean health care: What can hospitals learn from a world-class automaker? *Journal of Hospital Medicine (Online), 1*(3), 191–199. https://doi.org/10.1002/jhm.68.

Kim, Y., & Ballard, G. (2002). Earned value method and customer earned value. *Journal of Construction Research, 3*(1), 1–12. https://doi.org/10.1142/S1609945102000096.

Kozina, M., & Sekovanic, I. (2015). Using the Cobit 5 for E-health Governance. In *Central European Conference on Information and Intelligent System* (pp. 203–209). Retrieved from http://search.proquest.com/openview/35c02f049666b272cf70dfdff1ad87e7/1?pq-origsite=gscholar&cbl=1986354.

Kruskal, J. B., Reedy, A., Pascal, L., Rosen, M. P., & Boiselle, P. M. (2012). Lean approach to improving performance and Efficiency in a Radiology. *RadioGraphics, 32*(2), 573–588.

Kumar, S., & Aldrich, K. (2010). Overcoming barriers to electronic medical record (EMR) implementation in the US healthcare system: A comparative study. *Health Informatics Journal, 16*(4), 306–318. https://doi.org/10.1177/1460458210380523.

Kumar, S., Swanson, E., & Tran, T. (2009). RFID in the healthcare supply chain : Usage and application. *International Journal of Health Care Quality Assurance, 22*(1), 67–81. https://doi.org/10.1108/09526860910927961.

Lachman, P. (2013). Redefining the clinical gaze. *BMJ Quality and Safety, 22*(11), 888–890. https://doi.org/10.1136/bmjqs-2013-002322.

Leipzig, R. M., Sauvign, K., Granville, L. J., Harper, G. M., Kirk, L. M., Levine, S. A., … Fernandez, H. M. (2014). What is a geriatrician? American geriatrics society and association of directors of geriatric academic programs geriatric medicine. *Journal of American Geriatric Society, 62*, 924–929. https://doi.org/10.1111/jgs.12825.

Lewis, L., & Mann, S. (2014). *Engaging Frontline Staff in Real Time Improvement.*

Lindsey, G. (2017). The Journey to " Being Lean." Retrieved on April 1, 2019, from http://strategyhealthcare.com/the-journey-to-being-lean/.

Maarleveld, P. (2015). *Structured production planning and control using a push-pull hybrid approach.* Universiteit Twente.

Malavasi, M., & Schenetti, G. (2017). *Lean Manufacturing and Industry 4. 0 : an empirical analysis between Sustaining and Disruptive Change.* Politecnico di Milano.

Malpass, L. (2017). *Reducing Delays in Follow-up Care through Process Optimization.* University of San Francisco.

Mann, D. (2005). *Creating a Lean Culture: Tools to Sustain Lean Conversions.* New York: Productivity Press.

Mann, D. (2009). The missing link: Lean leadership. *Frontiers of Health Services Management, 26*(1), 15–26. https://doi.org/10.1097/01974520-200907000-00003.

Middleton, L. P., Price, K. M., Puig, P., Heydon, L. J., Tarco, E., Sneige, N., … Deavers, M. T. (2009). Implementation of American society of clinical oncology/College of American pathologists HER2 Guideline recommendations in a tertiary care facility increases HER2 immunohistochemistry and fluorescence in situ hybridization concordance and decreases the number of inconclusive cases. *Archives of Pathology & Laboratory Medicine, 133*, 775–780.

Mieczakowski, A., Goodman-deane, J., Patmore, J., & Clarkson, J. (2014). *Conversations, Conferencing and Collaboration: An Asia-Pacific Investigation of Factors Influencing the Effectiveness of Distributed Meetings.* London.

Miina, A. (2012). Lean problem: Why conpanies fail with lean implementation? *Management, 2*(5), 232–250. https://doi.org/10.5923/j.mm.20120205.12.

Miller, J. (2009). Visual Management Resource for Lean Hospitals. Retrieved on April 1, 2019, from https://blog.gembaacademy.com/2009/04/13/visual_management_resource_for_lean_hospitals_1/.

Moen, R. (2009). Foundation and History of the PDSA Cycle. In *Asian Network for Quality Conference* (pp. 2–10). Retrieved from https://www.deming.org/sites/default/files/pdf/2015/PDSA_History_Ron_Moen.pdf.

Moen, R., & Norman, C. (2009). Evolution of the PDCA Cycle. In *Proceedings of the 7th ANQ Congress*, Tokyo, 2009, September 17.

Morato, T. O. (2013). *Basis of a Procedural Model for Architecture-Engineering-Construction Industry*. Universitat Politècnica de València.

Moreno-Sanchez, D., Tijerina-Aguilera, J., Aguilar-Villarreal, A. Y., & Pilar-Tress, E. (2014). A systematic waste taxonomy for operational excellence implementation. In *IIE Annual Conference and Expo 2014* (pp. 3823–3831). Retrieved from http://www.scopus.com/inward/record.url?eid=2-s2.0-84910056478&partnerID=tZOtx3y1.

Mujtba, S., Feldt, R., Petersen, K., Mujtaba, S., & Ab, E. (2010). Waste and Lead Time Reduction in a Software Product Customization Process with Value Stream Maps. In *21st Australian Software Engineering Conference (ASWEC 2010)*, 6–9 April 2010, Auckland, New Zealand. IEEE Computer Society.

Nakane, J., & Hall, R. W. (2002). Ohno's method: Creating survival work culture. *Target, 18*(1), 6–15.

Nnamdi, M. C. (2015). *Enhancing Enterprise Resource Planning and Manufacturing Execution System Efficiency with Simulation-Based Decision Support*. University of Johannesburg.

Novartis. (2019). Lean Lab Design Workshop White Paper. Retrieved on April 1, 2019, from https://www.flad.com/content/epubs /Novartis_BSM_LeanLabDesignWo rkshopWhitePaper.pdf?132.

Oh, H. (1999). Service quality, customer satisfaction, and customer value: A holistic perspective. *Hospitality Management, 18*, 67–82. https://doi.org/10.1016/S0278-4319(98)00047-4.

Ojutkangas, A. (2016). *Establishing Process Management: Case Billerudkorsnas Finland Oy*. Tampere University.

Olson, G. M., & Olson, J. S. (2000). Dist2ance matters. *Human-Computer Interaction, 15*(2–3), 139–178. https://doi.org/10.1207/S15327051HCI153_4.

Phumchusri, N., & Panyavai, T. (2014). Electronic Kanban system for rubber seals production. *Engineering Journal, 19*(1), 37–50. https://doi.org/10.4186/ej.2015.19.1.37.

Poksinska, B., Swartling, D., & Drotz, E. (2013). The daily work of Lean leaders - lessons from manufacturing and healthcare. *Total Quality Management and Business Excellence, 24*(7–8), 886–898. https://doi.org/10.1080/14783363.2013.791098.

Portioli-Staudacher, A. (2008). Lean healthcare. An experience in Italy. *IFIP International Federation for Information Processing, 257*, 485–492. https://doi.org/10.1007/978-0-387-77249-3_50.

Powell, A., Piccoli, G., & Ives, B. (2004). Virtual teams: A review of current literature and directions for future research. *ACM SIGMIS Database, 35*(1), 6–36. https://doi.org/10.1145/968464.968467.

Prasad, K., & Akhilesh, K. B. (2002). Global virtual teams: What impacts their design and performance? *Team Performance Management: An International Journal, 8*, 102–112. https://doi.org/10.1108/13527590210442212.

Pries, L. (2004). *New Production Systems and Workers' Participation – a contradiction? Some Lessons from German Automobile Companies.*

Putri, L. R., & Susanto. (2017). Lean hospital approach to identify critical waste in the outpatient pharmacy instalation of RSI PKU Muhammadiyah Pekajangan. *Jurnal Medicoeticolegal Dan Manajemen Rumah Sakit, 6*(2), 163–173. https://doi.org/10.18196/jmmr.6139.

Qamar, A. (2011). *An Integrated Approach towards Model-Based Mechatronic Design.* KTH School of Industrial Engineering and Management.

Radnor, Z. J., Holweg, M., & Waring, J. (2012). Institutional repository lean in healthcare: The unfilled promise? *Social Science & Medicine, 75*(3), 364–371. https://doi.org/10.1021/acsphotonics.7b00904.

Redzic, C., & Baik, J. (2006). Six Sigma Approach in Software Quality Improvement. In *Fourth International Conference on Software Engineering Research, Management and Applications (SERA'06)* (pp. 396–406). https://doi.org/10.1109/SERA.2006.61.

Regina Qu'Appelle Health Region. (2015). *Better Everyday: Visual Management.*

Ribeiro, L., Alves, A. C., Moreira, J. F. P., & Ferreira, M. (2009). Applying Standard Work in a Paint Shop of Wood Furniture Plant: A Case Study. In *22nd International Conference on Production Research.* Challenges for Sustainable Operations (ICPR 22). Iguassu Falls-Brazil, 2013, 9p. CD-ROM. ISBN: 978-85-88478-47-3.

Román, L. F. (2009). *A Case of Acquisition, Transmission and Use of Information to Control a Manufacturing Process.* Universitat Politècnica de Catalunya. https://doi.org/10.1007/BF03192151.

Saad, N. M., Al-Ashaab, A., Maksimovic, M., Zhu, L., Shehab, E., Ewers, P., & Kassam, A. (2013). A3 thinking approach to support knowledge- driven design. *The International Journal of Advanced Manufacturing Technology, 68*(5), 1371–1386. Retrieved from https://dspace.lib.cranfield.ac.uk/bitstream/1826/10473/1/A3_thinking_approach_to_support_knowledge-driven_design-2013.pdf.

Sandholtz, K. (2012). Making standards stick : A theory of coupled vs. decoupled compliance. *Organization Studies, 33*(5–6), 655–679.

Schleyer, A. M., Robinson, E., Dumitru, R., Taylor, M., Hayes, K., Pergamit, R., … Cuschieri, J. (2016). Preventing hospital-acquired venous thromboembolism: Improving patient safety with interdisciplinary teamwork, quality improvement analytics, and data transparency. *Journal of Hospital Medicine, 11*, S38–S43. https://doi.org/10.1002/jhm.2664.

Simpeh, E. K. (2012). *An Analysis of the Causes and Impact of Rework in Construction Projects.* Cape Peninsula University of Technology.

Siren, T. (2008). *A Model for Product Transfer Project.* Lappeenranta University of Technology.

Sisson, J., & Elshennawy, A. (2015). Achieving success with Lean: An analysis of key factors in Lean transformation at Toyota and beyond. *International Journal of Lean Six Sigma, 6*(3), 263–280. https://doi.org/10.1108/IJLSS-07-2014-0024.

Smith, G., Poteat-Godwin, A., Harrison, L. M., & Randolph, G. D. (2012). Applying lean principles and kaizen rapid improvement events in public health practice. *Journal of Public Health Management Practice, 18*(1), 52–54. https://doi.org/10.1097/PHH.0b013e31823f57c0.

Sobanski, E. B. (2009). *Assessing Lean Warehousing: Development and Validation of Alean Assessment Tool.* Oklahoma State University. Retrieved from https://shareok.org/handle/11244/7781.

Spivey, J. (2018). Process improvement model A3 to reduce HAIs: Looking through a different lens. *Prevention Strategist, 11*(4), 66–69.

Sunder, V. M. (2016). Lean Six Sigma in higher education institutions. *International Journal of Quality & Reliability Management, 8*(2), 159–178.

Sung, J. (2018). *Breaking Through the Crisis: Toyota's Innovative Actions in Gemba.* Seoul National University.

Terfie, G. (2018). *The Effect of Kaizen Implementation on Organizational Performance of a Service Provider Public Institution the Case of Ethiopian Management Institute.* St. Mary University.

Thor, J. (2007). *Getting going on Getting Better: How is Systematic Quality Improvement Established in a Healthcare Organization? Implications for Change Management Theory and Practice.* Karolinska Institutet. Retrieved from http://diss.kib.ki.se/2007/978-91-7357-274-3%5Cnhttp://diss.kib.ki.se/2007/978-91-7357-274-3 TS - RIS.

Tohidi, H., & Liraviasl, K. K. (2012). Six sigma methodology and its relationship with lean manufacturing system. *Advances in Environmental Biology, 6*(2), 895–906.

Tribelsky, E., & Sacks, R. (2010). Measuring information flow in the detailed design of construction projects. *Research in Engineering Design, 21*(3), 189–206. https://doi.org/10.1007/s00163-009-0084-3.

Trueman, J. L. (2009). *Is EHR the Cure? An Examination of the Implementation of an Electronic Health Record in Rural Alberta.* University of Alberta.

Vaanila, T. (2015). *Process Development Using the Lean Six Sigma Methodology - Case: Oy AGA Ab, Linde Healthcare.* Hame University of Applied Science.

Valente, C. P., Pivatto, M. P., & Formoso, C. T. (2016). Visual Management: Preliminary Results of a Systematic Literature Review on Core Concepts and Principles. In *Proceedings 24th Annual Conference of the International Group for Lean Construction* (Vol. 55, pp. 123–132). Boston.

Venkateswaran, S. (2011). *Implementing Lean in Healthcare Warehouse Operations - Evaluation of 5S Best Practice.* Louisiana State University.

Ward, S. A., & McElwee, A. (2007). Application of the Principle of Batch Size Reduction in Construction. In *Lean Construction: A New Paradigm for Managing Capital Projects - 15th IGLC Conference* (pp. 539–548). Retrieved from http://www.scopus.com/inward/record.url?eid=2-s2.0-57749115326&partnerID=tZOtx3y1.

Waren, J. (2013). Lean Daily Management, Visual Management and Continuous Improvement. Lappeenranta University of Technology.

Williams, E., Fritz, P., Lovejoy, A., & Ed, M. (2014). *WY Infection Prevention Orientation Manual.*

Wilson, K. A., Burke, C. S., Priest, H. A., & Salas, E. (2005). Promoting health care safety through training high reliability teams. *Quality and Safety in Health Care, 14*(4), 303–309. https://doi.org/10.1136/qshc.2004.010090.

Wiseman, L. M. (2011). *Evaluating the Effectiveness and Efficiency of Continuous Improvement Training.* Oregon State University.

Worley, J. M. (2004). *The Role of Sociocultural Factors in a Lean Manufacturing Implementation.* Oregon State University.

Yalcindag, S. (2014). *Human Resource Planning Models for Home Health Care Services: Assignment and Routing Problems.* Politecnico di Milano.

Yankelovich, N., Walker, W., Roberts, P., Wessler, M., Kaplan, J., & Provino, J. (2004). Meeting central: making distributed meetings more effective. In *Proceedings of the 2004 ACM Conference on Computer Supported Cooperative Work* pp. 419–428. https://doi.org/10.1145/1031607.1031678.

Yee, T. S., Zain, Z. B. M., & Sin, T. C. (2017). An Engineering Approach to Increase Chances of Data Capture-ability and Data Analyzability in Work Measurement Practices. In *Proceedings of the 2017 International Symposium on Industrial Engineering and Operations Management (IEOM)* (pp. 192–202). Bristol.

Young, F. Y. F. (2014). The use of 5S in healthcare services: A literature review. *International Journal of Business and Social Science, 5*(101), 240–248.

Zarbo, R. J., Varney, R. C., Copeland, J. R., Angelo, R. D., Sharma, G., & Sam, C. M. E. (2015). Daily management system of the henry ford production system: QTIPS to focus continuous improvements at the level of the work. *American Journal of Clinical Pathology, 144*, 122–136. https://doi.org/10.1309/AJCPLQYMOFWU31CK.

Index

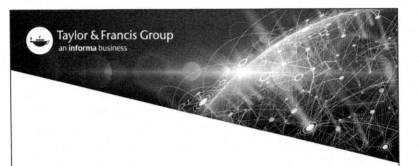

Printed in the United States
By Bookmasters